MADE
FOR
THIS

MADE FOR THIS

INSPIRING MESSAGES FOR WOMEN

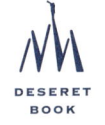

DESERET BOOK

Salt Lake City, Utah

Interior images: Oleksandra / Adobe Stock

© 2025 Brigham Young University

All rights reserved. No part of this book may be reproduced in any form or by any means without permission in writing from the publisher, Deseret Book Company, at permissions@deseretbook.com. This work is not an official publication of The Church of Jesus Christ of Latter-day Saints. The views expressed herein are the responsibility of the authors and do not necessarily represent the position of the Church or of Deseret Book Company.

DESERET BOOK is a registered trademark of Deseret Book Company.

Visit us at deseretbook.com

Library of Congress Cataloging-in-Publication Data

CIP on file
ISBN 978-1-63993-392-1

Printed in China
RR Donnelley, Dongguan, China

10 9 8 7 6 5 4 3 2 1

CONTENTS

YOU WERE BORN TO LEAD,
   YOU WERE BORN FOR GLORY 1
   Sheri Dew

REVELATION AND YOU 21
   Kate Holbrook

IN THIS LIFE, I WILL CHOOSE JOY 33
   Sunny Mahe

THROUGH THE WILDERNESS 45
   Tammy Uzelac Hall

WEBS OF FRIENDSHIP 57
   Ardeth G. Kapp

JESUS CHOOSES THE UNEXPECTED
   AS HIS MESSENGERS 63
   Shima Baughman

CONTENTS

BELIEVING AND BELONGING IN A BIG, BROKEN WORLD 77
Melissa Inouye

UNITING FAMILIES THROUGH TEMPLE WORK 93
Jihae Kwon

THE MIDDLE OF THE STORY 105
Sarah Sun

I WILL TRUST IN THEE FOREVER 115
Jennifer Kerns Davis

BECOMING WOMEN OF GREATER FAITH IN CHRIST 131
Patricia T. Holland

WE ARE HERE TO HAVE JOY 147
Lisa Valentine Clark

It doesn't take a lot of living to know that life can be tough. As babies, we struggled to learn how to be humans: how to move and speak and exist in this world. Now, older, we have harder lessons to learn: how to make wise decisions, how to handle disagreements, how to be good people (especially when things are difficult or sad or boring).

Even when we have faith in God and deeply believe that He is looking out for us, even when things are going well, sometimes we may find ourselves asking if we're *really* here for a reason. Is this life the one we're meant to be living? Are the schools we attended or the jobs we've had or the neighborhoods we've lived in the right ones, or have our unwitting actions somehow messed up God's perfect plan for us? Sometimes, we just need someone to remind us, like Mordecai reminded Esther, "Who knoweth whether thou art come to the kingdom for such a time as this?" (Esther 4:14).

In this book you will find testimony and advice from women like you—women of faith, from all walks of life, who have learned for themselves that God has put them here for a reason, just as He did with Esther and as He has with you. Each chapter is accompanied by a scripture passage from the book of Esther. As Esther discovers her divine destiny, travels through low points and high points, and finally comes out on the other side of her trial with joy, so will you.

You were made for this—this life, *your* life, with all its difficulties and all its joys. You were made to relish and enjoy the highs just as much as you were prepared to weather and rise above the lows.

You are here for a reason.

You were made for this.

YOU WERE MADE FOR A REASON

Then said the king's servants that ministered unto him . . . gather together all the fair young virgins unto Shushan the palace. . . . And let the maiden which pleaseth the king be queen instead of Vashti. And the thing pleased the king; and he did so.

Now in Shushan the palace there was a certain Jew, whose name was Mordecai . . . and he brought up Hadassah, that is, Esther, his uncle's daughter: for she had neither father nor mother, and the maid was fair and beautiful; whom Mordecai, when her father and mother were dead, took for his own daughter. (Esther 2:2–5, 7)

YOU WERE BORN TO LEAD, YOU WERE BORN FOR GLORY

Sheri Dew

SHERI DEW is a native of Ulysses, Kansas, and a graduate of Brigham Young University. She is the author of many books, including *Prophets See Around Corners* and biographical works on Presidents Russell M. Nelson, Gordon B. Hinckley, and Ezra Taft Benson. She served in the Relief Society General Presidency and is executive vice president and chief content officer of Deseret Management Corporation.

I went out to my car one evening to find the passenger window smashed and my briefcase stolen with everything in it—money, credit cards, all of my ID (including the passport that had taken me to fifty countries), and irreplaceable documents. Hoping the thieves had stolen the money and discarded everything else, a friend and I spent all night prowling through area dumpsters, hoping to find something. But we found nothing.

The next day I began the tedious process of replacing the

contents. Then, unexpectedly, two mornings later, my phone rang at 3:00 a.m. It was a Church operator.

"Sister Dew, did you lose a briefcase?"

"Yes," I answered.

"I have a man on the line who says he found it in a dumpster behind a bar. Been to any bars lately, Sister Dew?" Laughing at her own joke, she connected me with this man whose pickup, as it turned out, had been robbed that night and who had been going through dumpsters. In one he had found a briefcase. *My briefcase.* When I asked how he had tracked me down, he replied, "When I looked inside the briefcase and saw that Mormon recommendation, I knew this must be important."

He was referring, of course, to my temple recommend.

The phrase *Mormon recommendation* instantly reminded me of Mormon's tender words to his son Moroni: "I recommend thee unto God, and I trust in Christ that thou wilt be saved" (Moroni 9:22). I have often pondered what it would mean to be recommended to God.

In essence, every time we qualify for a temple recommend, our priesthood leaders are doing just that. But on this subject of recommendation there is another dimension to consider. For God our Father and His Son Jesus Christ, with Their perfect foreknowledge, already recommended every one of you to fill your mortal probation during the most decisive period in the history of the world. You are here now because you were elected to be here now (see 1 Peter 1:2).

You have been told countless times that you are a chosen generation reserved for the latter part of the latter days. President

Gordon B. Hinckley said, "You are the best generation we have ever had."[1] It's akin to being chosen to run the last leg of a relay, where the coach always positions his strongest runner.

You were recommended to help run the last leg of the relay that began with Adam and Eve because your premortal spiritual valor indicated you would have the courage and the determination to face the world at its worst, to do combat with the evil one during his heyday, and, in spite of it all, to be fearless in building the kingdom of God.

You simply *must* understand this, because you were born to lead by virtue of who you are, the covenants you have made, and the fact that you are here now in the eleventh hour. *You were born to lead,* and, in the words of Isaiah, *you were born for glory* (see Isaiah 62:2–3).

Now, the glorious but sobering truth is that, in spite of your eons of premortal preparation, if you've hoped to passively, comfortably live out your lives, let me burst that little bubble once and for all. Now, please, do not misunderstand me: This is a magnificent time to live! It is a time, said President Spencer W. Kimball, when our influence "can be tenfold what it might be in more tranquil times."[2] The strongest runner *wants* to run the last leg of the relay.

But the last days are not for the faint of heart or the spiritually out of shape. There will be days when you feel defeated, exhausted, and plain old beat-up by life's whiplash. People you love will disappoint you—and you will disappoint them. Some days it will feel as though the veil between heaven and earth is made of reinforced concrete. And you may even face a crisis of faith. In fact, you can count on trials that test your testimony and your faith.

Aren't you glad I come bearing such optimistic news? Actually, I am nothing if not optimistic about you, for everything about your lives is an indicator of our Father's remarkable respect for you. Now is the day when His kingdom is being established once and for all, never again to be taken from the earth. This is the last leg of the relay. This is when He needs His strongest runners.

The simple fact is that our Father did not recommend Eve or Moses or Nephi or countless other magnificent exemplars for this dispensation—He recommended you and me. Do you think God would have left the last days to chance by sending men and women He couldn't count on? Happily, though we must each walk through life on our own, we don't have to do it alone. Four principles explain why:

First, God wants a powerful people.

Second, He gives His power to those who are faithful.

Third, we have a sacred obligation to seek after the power of God and then to use that power as He directs.

Fourth, when we have the power of God with us, nothing is impossible.

I repeat, God wants a powerful people. Ammon taught that "a man may have great *power* given him from God" (Mosiah 8:16; emphasis added), and Nephi prophesied that we of the latter days would be "armed with . . . the *power* of God in great glory" (1 Nephi 14:14; emphasis added).

There are many evidences that God wants a powerful people. This is one reason that at baptism we become eligible to receive "the gift and the power of the Holy Ghost" (1 Nephi 13:37) and the privilege of constant access to the third member of the Godhead.

This is one reason *every* worthy adult may go to the temple, from which he or she emerges surrounded and protected by God's power (see Doctrine and Covenants 109:22).

God wants a powerful people. No one better understands that Satan is real and that he has power. No one better understands that none of us is smart enough or resilient enough to spar with Satan and survive spiritually. Where there is any kind of dishonesty, immorality, contention, or addiction, there is Satan. And he will devour you—unless you "put on the whole armour [or power] of God" (Ephesians 6:11), for the power of God is stronger than the power of Satan.

If God wants a powerful people who can withstand the wiles of the devil—and He does—and if we were born to lead in these latter days—and we were—then we need to understand how God makes His power available to us and how we gain access to that power.

Number 1: There Is Power in the Word of God

Alma and the sons of Mosiah learned that the preaching of the word—meaning the gospel of Jesus Christ—has a "more powerful effect upon the minds of the people than . . . anything else" (Alma 31:5). There is power in the word to heal our wounded souls (see Jacob 2:8), to help us overcome temptation (see 1 Nephi 11:25), to prompt us to repent (see Jarom 1:12), to bring about a mighty change in our hearts (see Alma 5:13), and to lead us to Christ.

President Boyd K. Packer taught:

> True doctrine, understood, changes attitudes and behavior.

> The study of the doctrines of the gospel will improve behavior quicker than a study of behavior will improve behavior.[3]

In other words, the word of God can transform us.

I have a lifelong friend whose teenage tampering with pornography evolved, and for years it ruled him and ravaged his marriage. Then, a remarkable sequence of events began to unfold. He began to study the scriptures for the first time since his mission. The word of God pierced his heart, and he knew he had to repent.

One day he wrote me this:

> It was when I began to study the gospel that I realized I had been under Satan's power for years. When I finally got on my knees, pleaded for help to change, and surrendered my sins to the Lord, my world turned upside down. . . . I wish I could tell everyone who is in a situation like I was to not be afraid to surrender to the Lord. They will find joy like never before in His Atonement. They will feel the Father wrap His arms around them. They will discover there is power in the gospel to really change.

The gospel has the power to cleanse and make new, because the word "is quick and powerful," it "divide[s] asunder all the cunning . . . of the devil," and it "lead[s] the man of Christ" home (Helaman 3:29). The Atonement is real. My friend is evidence of that. His great change is the change that comes with conversion.

In the spring of 2003, I spent two weeks at the United Nations as a White House delegate to an international commission. As I listened to women from around the world debate complex social problems, I didn't hear them raise one issue that couldn't be solved by living the gospel. Not one.

There is power in the word.

Number 2: There Is Power in the Gift of the Holy Ghost

The gift of the Holy Ghost is a gift of power. The Holy Ghost inspires and heals, guides and warns, enhances our natural capacities, inspires charity and humility, strengthens us during trials, testifies of the Father and the Son, and shows us "all things" that we should do (2 Nephi 32:5).

Because the Holy Ghost will show us everything we should do, it only makes sense to learn how He communicates—or to learn the language of revelation.

I remember a time when I was desperate for guidance on a crucial decision. I had fasted and prayed and been to the temple, but the answer wasn't clear. In frustration I told a friend that I just couldn't get an answer. He responded, simply: "Have you asked the Lord to teach you how He communicates with you?" I hadn't, so I began to pray daily that He would.

Not long thereafter, while reading about Nephi building the ship, I couldn't help but notice how clearly he understood the Lord's instructions. With that, I began to hunt for scriptural evidences of direct communication between God and man. At each one I made a little red x in the margin of my scriptures. Now, many years later, my scriptures are littered with little red x's, each an indication that the Lord does communicate with His people—and often. The scriptures are the handbook for the language of revelation. If you will regularly immerse yourself in the scriptures, you'll get clearer, more frequent answers to your prayers.

Learning this language takes time. As a young captain charged with leading the Nephite armies, Moroni sent messengers to the prophet Alma, asking him to inquire of the Lord where the armies should go. But in time Moroni received inspiration for his stewardship himself, for he became "a man of a perfect understanding" (Alma 48:11)—suggesting that he learned to speak the language of revelation, perhaps even perfectly.

What a gift to have access to a pure source of information, a source devoid of flattery or spin-doctoring, "for the Spirit speaketh the truth and lieth not" (Jacob 4:13). The Lord will teach us directly as much truth as we are worthy and willing to learn.

Having the Holy Ghost as our constant guide and protector is essential to latter-day leadership, for the gift of the Holy Ghost is a gift of power.

Number 3: There Is Power in the Priesthood

By definition, priesthood power is the power and authority of God delegated to men on earth. Those who hold the priesthood have the right to say what the Lord would say if He were here. Whatever they bind on earth is bound in heaven.

Because the priesthood was restored, we have access to ordinances: baptism and confirmation, sealings and healings and blessings, miracles, and the ministering of angels. Indeed, "the keys of *all* the spiritual blessings of the church" (Doctrine and Covenants 107:18; emphasis added) are available through the power and authority of the Melchizedek Priesthood.

There is *power* in ordinances. All who are baptized and receive the Holy Ghost are eligible to speak the words of Christ and qualify for eternal life. Those who are endowed with power in the house of the Lord need never face the adversary alone. Couples worthy to be sealed in that holy house are gifted with power. The power of the priesthood heals, protects, and inoculates every righteous man and woman against the powers of darkness. I am deeply grateful for the power of the priesthood and the gift of having full access to this power, which when used righteously is the only true power on earth.

Number 4: There Is Power in the House of the Lord

It is precisely because of priesthood power—the fulness of which is available only in the temple—that we may be endowed with power in the house of the Lord. The Prophet Joseph Smith made this clear at the Kirtland Temple dedication, when he prayed "that thy servants may go forth from this house armed with thy power" (Doctrine and Covenants 109:22).

For years now I have attended the temple frequently. It is a place of refuge and revelation. One year, however, a head-banging, hand-wringing challenge drove me to attend even more. There were weeks when the only peace I felt was in the temple. Even still, after about six months, nine words from 1 Nephi leapt off the page: "And I, Nephi, did go into the mount oft" (1 Nephi 18:3). Instantly I knew I needed to spend even more time in the temple. So I did.

The results were not what I expected. Although I received help with the challenge in question, it seems that the Lord simply needed me to be in the temple more, where it is easier to learn certain things. That was apparently Nephi's experience as well, for as he went "into the mount oft," the Lord "showed unto [him] great things"—undoubtedly great things of the Spirit.

In the temple we learn how to deal with Satan, how to live in the world without letting it stain us, how to fulfill our foreordained missions, and how to come into the presence of God. Our kept covenants will eventually save us. And that is power!

Number 5: There Is Power in the Atonement of Jesus Christ

Until I was in my thirties, I thought the Atonement of Jesus Christ was basically for sinners—meaning that it allowed us to repent. But then I suffered a heartbreaking personal loss and began to learn that there was so much more to this sublime doctrine.

My solution initially to my heartbreak was to exercise so much faith that the Lord would have to give me what I wanted—which was a husband. Believe me, if fasting and prayer and temple attendance automatically resulted in a husband, I'd have one.

The Lord hasn't even yet given me a husband; but He did heal my heart. And in doing so, He taught me that He not only paid the price for sin but compensated for all of the pain we experience in life. He taught me that because of His Atonement, we have access to His grace, or enabling power—power that frees us from sin; power to be healed emotionally, physically, and spiritually; power to "loose the bands of death" (Alma 7:12); power to turn weakness into strength (see Ether 12:27); and power to receive salvation through faith on His name (see Mosiah 3:19). It is because of the

Atonement that, if we build our foundation on Christ, the devil can have no power over us (see Helaman 5:12).

There is power in God the Father and His Son Jesus Christ—power that we may access through the word, the Holy Ghost, the priesthood, and the ordinances of the holy temple.

What then must we do to access this power? May I suggest three things?

First of all, have faith.

Faith is the first principle of the gospel because faith is a principle of power that influences, to at least some degree, the Lord's intervention in our lives.

"So great was the faith of [the previously insecure] Enoch that . . . he spake the word of the Lord, and the earth trembled, and the mountains fled" (Moses 7:13). So great was the faith of the fourteen-year-old Joseph that when he went into a grove of trees and asked "in faith, nothing wavering" (James 1:6), the Father and the Son appeared, ushering in the Restoration.

Faith is a principle of power, which explains why President Hinckley repeatedly declared: "If there is any one thing you and I need in this world it is faith."[4]

Soon after President Hinckley was called to serve as a counselor to President Spencer W. Kimball, the health of the prophet and his two other counselors failed, leaving President Hinckley to shoulder the burdens of the presidency alone. At one point he recorded:

> The responsibility I carry frightens me. . . . Sometimes I could weep with concern. But there comes the assurance that the Lord put me here for His purpose, and if I will be

humble and seek the direction of the Holy Spirit, He will use me . . . to accomplish His purposes.[5]

Throughout his life, President Hinckley's practice was to simply go forward with faith.

Prophets ancient and modern stand as witnesses that the Lord will indeed use His matchless power to help us. Surely the brother of Jared's transcendent privilege of seeing the Lord was linked to his expression of faith:

> I know, O Lord, that thou hast all power, and can do whatsoever thou wilt for the benefit of man; therefore touch these stones. . . .
> . . . O Lord, thou canst do this. (Ether 3:4–5)

In this instance, as in many others, faith allowed the Lord to do not just what was asked of Him, but much more.

If your faith is wobbly, if you're not sure the Lord will come to your aid, experiment, put Him to the test: "Even if ye can no more than desire to believe, let this desire work in you" (Alma 32:27). A great place to start is in the scriptures. As Jacob wrote: "We search the prophets, and we have many revelations . . . ; and having all these witnesses we obtain a hope, and our faith becometh unshaken" (Jacob 4:6).

Unshaken faith activates the power of God in our lives, "for he worketh by power, according to the faith of the children of men" (Moroni 10:7).

Second, we can increase our access to godly power through repentance and obedience.

Faith in Jesus Christ leads us to repent—or turn away from

sins that hold us spiritually captive—and to obey with exactness. Great power follows those who repent and obey.

Lamoni's father pledged to "give away" *all* his sins to know God (Alma 22:18). I invite you to do the same. What favorite sins, large or small, are you willing to give away—right now, today—to increase your access to the power of God?

It is not possible to sin enough to be happy. It is not possible to buy enough to be happy or to entertain or indulge yourself enough to be happy. Happiness and joy come only when you are living up to who you are. King Benjamin clearly understood this when he admonished us:

> Consider on the blessed and happy state of those that keep the commandments of God. For . . . they are blessed in all things . . . ; and if they hold out faithful to the end . . . they may dwell with God in a state of never-ending happiness. (Mosiah 2:41)

Satan no doubt bristles at this principle, for happiness is something the ultimate narcissist will never experience. I have yet to meet the man or woman who is happier because he or she was dishonest or because they were addicted to something or because they were immoral. It is so much easier to be righteous than to sin.

One summer I was invited to speak on the subject of the family to a gathering of United Nations diplomats. I agonized over what to say to such a diverse group. In the end I simply shared my personal experience. I explained that my parents had taught me as a child that personal virtue was essential for a happy marriage and family and that in my youth I had made promises to God that I would live a chaste life.

I then acknowledged that I was about to turn fifty and that, though I had not yet married, I had kept my promise. "It hasn't always been easy to stay morally clean," I admitted, "but it has been far easier than the alternative. I have never spent one second worrying about an unwanted pregnancy or disease. I have never had a moment's anguish because a man used and then discarded me. And when I do marry, I will do so without regret. So you see," I concluded, "I believe a moral life is actually an easier and a happier life."

I worried about how this sophisticated audience would respond to a message about virtue and abstinence, but much to my surprise they leapt to their feet in applause—not because of me but because the Spirit had borne witness of the truth of that message.

The happiest people I know are those who repent regularly and obey. They have increased their access to the power of God.

Third, to increase the power of God in our lives we must diligently seek.

There is perhaps no more frequent invitation or reassuring promise in all of scripture than this one: "Seek me diligently and ye shall find me; ask, and ye shall receive; knock, and it shall be opened unto you" (Doctrine and Covenants 88:63).

Notice that God never said, "Seek me a zillion times. Beg again and again and, maybe, just maybe, if you're lucky, I'll help you a little." To the contrary, the two greatest of all beings are ever ready to help us—no call waiting, no voicemail.

Most of the revelations received by the Prophet Joseph Smith came after diligent seeking, including this magnificent promise:

> I, the Lord, . . . delight to honor those who serve me in righteousness. . . .
>
> Great shall be their reward and eternal shall be their glory.
>
> And to them will I reveal all mysteries. . . .
>
> And their wisdom shall be great, and their understanding reach to heaven. . . .
>
> For . . . by my power will I make known unto them the secrets of my will. (Doctrine and Covenants 76:5–10)

Clearly there is no limit to what the Lord is willing to teach and give us.

The question, then, for you and me is, how much power do we want to have, and what are we willing to do to obtain it? Heber C. Kimball said:

> The greatest torment [the Prophet Joseph] had . . . was because this people would not live up to their [spiritual] privileges. . . . He said . . . he felt . . . as though he were pent up in an acorn shell, and all because the people . . . would not prepare themselves to receive the rich treasures of wisdom and knowledge that he had to impart. He could have revealed a great many things to us if we had been ready.[6]

Spiritual privileges that call forth the powers of heaven are available to all who diligently seek them. God wants a powerful people; but, again, how much power we learn to access is up to each of us.

The question, then, is: Will you diligently seek? Listen to this classic passage from Alma: "Whosoever will come may come and partake of the waters of life freely; and whosoever will not come the same is not compelled to come" (Alma 42:27). Notice that this passage doesn't say that just the popular ones or the smart ones on full scholarship or the ones who got married at twenty-one may come. It says "whosoever will"—meaning it is our choice.

In his last major address as prime minister, and while World War II still raged in the Pacific, Winston Churchill said this to his countrymen:

> I told you hard things at the beginning of [this war]; you did not shrink, and I should be unworthy of your confidence . . . if I did not still cry: Forward, unflinching, unswerving, indomitable, till the whole task is done and the whole world is safe and clean.[7]

I told you hard things. But I've also shared reassurance that if you will learn to draw upon the power of God, you will not shrink. You will go forward, making the world safer and cleaner until you've done everything you were born to do. For you were born to lead. You were born to build Zion. You were born for glory.

In conclusion, in the words of Moroni, "I would commend you to seek this Jesus of whom the prophets and apostles have written" (Ether 12:41) so that you experience for yourself the power in Jesus Christ to strengthen you, to sanctify you, and to help you run this leg of the relay. Don't ever underestimate the power of Jesus Christ to help you. Isaiah said it this way:

> Hast thou not known? hast thou not heard, that the everlasting God, the Lord, the Creator of the ends of the earth, fainteth not, neither is weary? . . .
>
> He giveth power to the faint; and to them that have no might he increaseth strength. . . .
>
> . . . They that wait upon the Lord shall renew their strength; they shall mount up with wings as eagles; they shall run, and not be weary; and they shall walk, and not faint. (Isaiah 40:28–31)

I have learned for myself that this is true—that because of our Father and His Son, we don't have to run this last strenuous leg of the relay alone. We have access to the greatest and grandest of all power. And when we have the power of God with us, we truly can do all things—including everything we were born to do. And we were born to lead. We were born for glory.

NOTES

Adapted from a devotional address given at BYU.

1. Gordon B. Hinckley, "An Ensign to the Nations, a Light to the World," *Ensign,* November 2003.
2. Spencer W. Kimball, "Privileges and Responsibilities of Sisters," *Ensign,* November 1978.
3. Boyd K. Packer, "Little Children," *Ensign,* November 1986.
4. Gordon B. Hinckley, "God Shall Give unto You Knowledge by His Holy Spirit," *Speeches of the Year, 1973* (Provo, UT: Brigham Young University, 1974), 109.

5. In Sheri Dew, *Go Forward with Faith: The Biography of Gordon B. Hinckley* (Salt Lake City: Deseret Book, 1996), 393.
6. Heber C. Kimball in *Journal of Discourses*, 10:167.
7. "Forward, Till the Whole Task Is Done," London BBC radio broadcast, 13 May 1945, in *Blood, Toil, Tears and Sweat: The Speeches of Winston Churchill,* ed. David Cannadine (Boston: Houghton Mifflin, 1989), 266.

YOU WERE MADE FOR GRACE

So it came to pass, when the king's commandment and his decree was heard, and . . . Esther was brought also unto the king's house. . . . And the maiden pleased him, and she obtained kindness of him.

Esther had not shewed her people nor her kindred: for Mordecai had charged her that she should not shew it. . . .

And the king loved Esther above all the women, and she obtained grace and favour in his sight more than all the virgins; so that he set the royal crown upon her head, and made her queen instead of Vashti. (Esther 2:8–10, 17)

REVELATION AND YOU

Kate Holbrook

KATE HOLBROOK (1972–2022) was a leading voice in the study of Latter-day Saint women. She held a BA from Brigham Young University, an MTS from Harvard Divinity School, and a PhD from Boston University. Kate was a Specialist in Women's History, Managing Historian of Women's History, and Academic Outreach Director at the Church History Department of The Church of Jesus Christ of Latter-day Saints.

First Vision

When Joseph Smith went to the woods to pray one spring day, he was not yet a prophet. At that point, he was a boy who read his Bible and sought earnestly for the gospel. He felt eager to know God's will. Some important messages come from the First Vision. One of them is that family, status, education, wealth, and maturity are not the things God takes into account when deciding whom to speak with. Not only does it not matter where your parents went to college, it doesn't matter whether they went to college or whether they can read. And those things don't matter about you, either. Are you out of money? Not relevant. Do you share a bed with your siblings? Doesn't matter.

This is good news for those who throughout history often had less access to institutional religious authority. For many women in the world, for example, interaction with God has felt out of reach because it was associated most often with men and priestly office. But the First Vision and the Restored Gospel provide a balance to that—Joseph Smith was in his early teens when he prayed and he wasn't ordained to any priesthood. Instead, he was a person who learned from the scriptures and had enough faith to pray and ask for answers. We do that, too. Although we aren't called by God to restore the fullness of the gospel, God does call us and teach us to be more effective, wise, and loving—more like our parents in heaven.[1]

There is also a lot that the First Vision does not teach us. For example, it does not teach us about Relief Society, priesthood power, baptism, or temple ordinances. It does not teach us how often God will answer prayers or in what form.

One major lesson the First Vision does teach about revelation is that it is not the same thing as an instruction manual. Revelation can be slow, spotty, and take a while to figure out. In the words that I first heard from Sister Sharon Eubank: "Revelation is a process." I have found that when you stick with it, you can find treasure.

Revelation as a Process

When it takes a long time for an initial revelation to bear actual fruit, some of us can start to doubt our interpretation of the revelation. While it's good to be prayerfully open to the possibility that we have misunderstood something, it's also important to remember that revelation takes time. My study of Church history has taught me that our leaders have pursued their planning and decision-making "by study and also by faith." Revelation, study, and faith all interweave in the process.

I'll now share two examples from Church history showing how revelation is a process and is essential to the continuing restoration of the church.

Living in Farmington, Utah, forty-three-year-old Aurelia Spencer Rogers noticed a problem. The boys were rowdy, inconsiderate, and apparently not grounded in the gospel that their elders had sacrificed security, comfort, and relationships to preserve. Remarkably, as Sister Rogers looked for solutions to this problem, God whispered to her His approval and encouragement, so she pursued her solutions, which have enriched Latter-day Saint lives around the world ever since.

First, Aurelia Rogers shared her ideas with Eliza R. Snow and other female leaders, who liked them and described them to acting Church president John Taylor. Soon, she had a mandate to gather the children in Farmington and to figure out how an organization for them should function. Looking back, she later described how she felt after accepting the calling:

> While thinking over what was to be done for the best good of the children, I seemed to be carried away in the Spirit, or at least I experienced a feeling of untold happiness which lasted three days and nights. During that time nothing could worry or irritate me; if my little ones were

fretful, or the work went wrong, I had patience, could control in kindness, and manage my household affairs easily.[2]

But those joyous feelings were not permanent. While planning and working for the children, she began to feel unworthy and depressed, so much so that she had trouble fulfilling her responsibilities. "I went to my meetings weeping by the way, being humbled to the very earth; so much so, that whatever anyone said afterward in my praise, did not make me feel exalted, or lifted up in my own mind."[3]

Nonetheless, she went on to found what we now call the Primary organization. Maybe you wonder, as I have, why she experienced this dark sadness while doing important work.

Shouldn't acting on revelation and being on the Lord's errand feel endlessly blissful? Shouldn't it keep negative feelings at bay? That would only be true if Eve and Adam had not eaten that special fruit. In real life, acting on revelation is not a promise that we will feel inspired all the time. We did not come to earth for easy. Being embodied is not easy and working with other people is not easy, but these are two of the major reasons we are here, to have the experience of inhabiting a mortal body and to work with and serve other people.

Just as for Aurelia Rogers acting on revelation did not yield uninterrupted happiness, acting on revelation does not promise that all the support we need will fall into place. Ardeth Kapp, whom you may remember as Young Women general president during the 1980s, had experience with this. Immediately after accepting this calling, she began to receive revelation. She wrote in her journal, "It seems to me the heavens are opening and thoughts, directions, spiritual promptings are coming clear and fast."[4] Even at that early time, she felt the organization needed a charter statement and a goal system that was based on values. But it took three years of focused effort before the Young Women theme and values were fully created and announced, and five years until the values-based Personal Progress manual came out. Collaboration, execution, and further revelation took time. So did getting approvals.

The program changes Sister Kapp oversaw were complicated and getting the details right was slow. There were delays, repetitive extra labor, and other frustrations. But the result was programs that effectively nurtured the young women of the Church for over thirty years. Sister Kapp's example motivates me because even when discouraged she continued to counsel with others, exercise faith, fast, pray, and work hard. When I read about her experiences, I feel the Spirit testify that she acted on revelation and that God magnified her considerable native talents through collaboration with other people. If we don't continue to pursue the Lord's guidance, particularly when we encounter difficulties or frustrations, then we might overlook inspired solutions and fail to fix problems. We and others may not learn what the Lord invites us to learn.

Our Revelations—Receiving and Recording

Now I'm going to shift from talking about others' revelations to talking about our own, especially how our revelations can help us be better at helping others. I have a quotation near my desk to remind me that good thinking and good work take time and careful study. The words are from Simone Weil, a French philosopher who thought a lot about right and wrong and who went to great personal sacrifice to live in the ways she thought were morally right.

Weil taught, "All wrong translations, all absurdities in geometry problems, all clumsiness of style and all faulty connection of ideas . . . all such things are due to the fact that thought has seized upon some idea too hastily and being thus prematurely blocked, is not open to truth."[5]

To make ourselves feel less vulnerable, we humans like to define things. We often grab onto a definition quickly, because having the definition makes us feel comfortable and safe. As Weil suggests, the problem with the speed is that we can reach a wrong conclusion. Excessive speed can also mean we teach a false principle in a lesson or argue on social media in a way that treats someone unfairly.

On the other hand, not everything needs to take a long time. Perfectionism can keep us from ever getting anything done. Bearing a simple testimony; studying the scriptures with another person; reaching out in ministry—these can be part of our process instead of a perfect end.

They can be imperfect. Prayers can be imperfect. We can be imperfect. In fact, in this life we try to improve, but we can't help but make mistakes. We will not be perfect in receiving revelation, either, because it is a process. Perfectionism can paralyze us and prevent us from accomplishing the good that can simply result from trying.

I'd like to acknowledge how painful it can feel when you don't feel adept at receiving and understanding revelation. There are valiant souls among us who obey and seek—who strive to do everything right—yet struggle with this. That situation can be upsetting.

They can feel unworthy, although they are not, isolated from God and from other members of the Church. I have mourned that even Mother Teresa, a devout and tremendous example of service and spiritual wisdom, felt for long periods that God was distant. In one case, she asked someone she trusted to pray for her, that she would do God's will when she herself couldn't hear God's will: "The silence and the emptiness is so great, that I look and do not see—Listen and do not hear. . . . I want you to pray for me—that I let Him have [a] free hand."[6]

So what do we do if we don't feel we receive answers to our prayers? Some people I admire deeply fall into this category, and I have learned from observing them.

First, they recognize that some of us have an easier time receiving and understanding revelation than others. Other gifts come more naturally to them, and the gifts they do have they use to serve others.

Next, they acknowledge all the goodness that comes from Church participation. They see the beautiful lives and relationships it fosters. They trust in its goodness. They continue to serve, pray, fast, and read their scriptures, even when they do not have strong spiritual feelings.

Finally, they are humble. They remember the moments when they have felt the influence of divine power, however slight. Instead of stomping their feet that they don't have more, they appreciate what they do have.

I also want to add a note of hope here. When they served in their respective Relief Society general presidencies, both Sheri Dew and Julie Beck taught that revelation is a skill we can develop. I believe that is true. I have watched a friend who doesn't believe that he has the gift of personal revelation, but generously serves anyway. I see thoughts come to him with increasing frequency to act in a particular way. He has learned to trust those thoughts, even if he can't be sure that they are personal revelation. He acts in faith and comes closer to God as a result. His life and those of many others have been enriched by his willingness to try.

These paths I've described are not my own. One of the great treasures of my life is the gift of personal revelation. Even so, this gift waxes and wanes. Some weeks I receive insights to remember and act on during several of my prayers. Some weeks I do not. Sometimes I receive less because I ask vague questions or I fail to listen. Other times I don't ask or listen well, and I receive direction anyway. And then there are periods when God needs me to work things out on my own. In all of these stages, I know that where I fall short, I can repent and God will forgive and also compensate others for my blunders. I trust that God is the architect of the final picture. Not all of us have the skills to easily understand revelation, but I believe even those of us who struggle with personal revelation can grow closer to God in the process of doing good work.

Revelation and the Gathering of Israel

Now let's spend some time on the relationship of revelation to the gathering of Israel. President Nelson has been encouraging the youth, and us, to participate in the gathering of Israel.[7] To my mind, the gathering of Israel means a blessing for the whole world as well as for Church members and potential Church members.

Passages written by the Book of Mormon prophet Nephi have

helped me to imagine more about what the gathering of Israel looks like. Nephi describes this time from the perspective of mortals: "he gathereth his children from the four quarters of the earth; and he numbereth his sheep, and they know him; and there shall be one fold and one shepherd; and he shall feed his sheep, and in him they shall find pasture" (1 Nephi 22:25). I love the image here of all of us, from every part of the earth, finding pasture together, under one perfect, all-loving shepherd. There is a pasture I love which I visit every summer. Horses and cows graze there, and deer. The sky, mountains, meadow, trees, and streams are beautiful. The air is clear. The animals have all that they need and they are safe there. To have all of us in a safe and beautiful place where we are known, seen, and cared for—I want to be in that place and I want to help others find it.

Revelation is crucial to the gathering of Israel. Seeking God's will is the way we can find pasture and help others to do so as well. I long to see all of us dwell safely with the Holy One of Israel, and that promise motivates me to pursue revelation so I can contribute to this process and help more of us to the pasture of Jesus.

Conclusion

Adopting a view of revelation as a process requires patience and hope. By definition, hope is something we have despite negative past experience or evidence that points to the contrary. Hope is something we choose. When you feel acutely one of the world's problems, you can spend all of your energy in anger and criticism, or you can study, pray, and choose to hope in the solution that comes, and in your role as part of the solution. Criticism is vital to good thinking, but I believe we must balance it with hope and with positive action. We can hold that hope out in front of us to light our way and to light the way of others.

James Christensen's painting *The Responsible Woman* has been meaningful to me for a long time. It shows a woman with items strapped all over her body. She appears to be flying. Of the things strapped to her body, so that she doesn't drop them, one of them is a baby. One of them is a rope. One of them is a musical instrument. I wonder whether that candle is the reason she can fly. Imagine yourselves as this woman. What is strapped to your body? To mine is strapped three daughters and a husband, but they also help me, so maybe we're all attached to each other by ropes extending out. I carry along a pen and paper. Books. A salad to deliver. A garden shovel. Someone else's baby because I like to help younger moms. A list of people to pray for. A vacuum cleaner. A folder of writing to edit. Esther Ackerberg's recipe for Swedish Pancakes. What, for you, would the flame be that you hold? For me, that candle is hope and all the things that make up that hope: the gospel of Jesus Christ as restored by Joseph Smith and woven into our church institution by every prophet since; Latter-day Saint women's experiences from the past two hundred years; my ancestors; my friends; and you. Fire is contagious, and others' flames keep mine burning.

We can do substantial good in this world not because doing so is simple, but because we are strong enough to do things that are hard. Our Heavenly Father is waiting to help us, to make us stronger. He needs us to follow through on answers to the questions He is waiting for us to ask.[8]

Sisters, we are endowed with godly power. Let's exercise that power to light this world with God's love.

NOTES

Adapted from a talk given at BYU Women's Conference.

1. "Our theology begins with heavenly parents. Our highest aspiration is to be like them." Dallin H. Oaks, "Apostasy and Restoration," *Ensign,* May 1995, 84.
2. Aurelia Spencer Rogers, *Life Sketches of Orson Spencer and Others: And History of Primary Work* (Salt Lake City: George Q. Cannon & Sons Co., 1898), 212.
3. Rogers, 214.
4. Ardeth G. Kapp and Carolyn J. Rasmus, interview by Gordon Irving, 1992, 41, Church History Library.
5. Simone Weil, *Waiting on God (Routledge Revivals)* (Routledge, 2009), 35.
6. David Van Biema, "Mother Teresa's Crisis of Faith," *Time,* August 23, 2007, https://time.com/4126238/mother-teresas-crisis-of-faith/.
7. "I'm extending a prophetic plea to you, the women of the Church, to shape the future by helping to gather scattered Israel," Russell M. Nelson, "Sisters' Participation in the Gathering of Israel," *Ensign*, November 2018; "'My dear extraordinary youth, you were sent to earth at this precise time, the most crucial time in the history of the world, to help gather Israel,' the prophet said," Charlotte Larcabal, "A Call to Enlist and Gather Israel," *New Era,* March 2019; "We gather pedigree charts, create family group sheets, and do temple work vicariously to gather individuals unto the Lord and into their families," Russell M. Nelson, "The Gathering of Scattered Israel," *Ensign*, November 2006.
8. "I do not think that God is insulted when we forget Him. Rather, I think He is deeply disappointed. He knows that we have deprived ourselves of the opportunity to draw closer to Him by remembering Him and His goodness. We then miss out on Him drawing nearer to us and the specific blessings He has promised." Dale G. Rendlund, "Consider the Goodness and Greatness of God," *Liahona,* May 2020.

YOU WERE MADE TO WITHSTAND HARD TIMES

And the letters were sent by posts into all the king's provinces, to destroy, to kill, and to cause to perish, all Jews, both young and old, little children and women, in one day . . . and to take the spoil of them for a prey. (Esther 3:13)

IN THIS LIFE, I WILL CHOOSE JOY

Sunny Mahe

SUNNY MAHE is a former BYU volleyball All-American, answers to the alias "Reno Mahe's wife," and is a mother of ten, including one three-year-old angel. She is a taxi driver of aspiring young athletes, a crafter, a Disney pin trader, and a singer of mediocre karaoke.

There is a popular movie that I watched as a kid where something really traumatic happens to the main character, so he runs away and some new friends teach him an African phrase that basically means, "Have you tried just not caring?" They even sing a catchy song about it.

I believe that toxic positivity, pretending, faking, and masking our sadness or pain is just a recipe for mental health challenges. It is healthier to work through the emotions than to try to pretend they don't exist. Now, as a disclaimer, if you are struggling through depression or anxiety, I weep with you and I pray you will find relief through receiving the best professional care. I do not claim to have any magic cure for warding off sadness, grief, or pain. But

I have found that the heights of joy we can expect to attain are directly correlated to the depths of sorrow and pain we have known. Or, in other words, our capacity for joy is equal to our capacity for sorrow, pain, and grief. We read in Alma 36:20, "Yea, my soul was filled with joy as exceeding as was my pain!"

I think this is good news. There is purpose for pain. It increases our capacity to feel even more joy! Perhaps you are in a painful chapter of your life right now. That's okay. Even the Savior of the world was described as "a man of sorrows, and acquainted with grief" (Isaiah 53:3). He wept (see John 11:35), and even said, "My soul is exceeding sorrowful unto death" (Mark 14:34). But ultimately, I don't think people think of Jesus as someone who was always unhappy or depressed. So how did Jesus endure to the end?

Let's look at Hebrews 12:2: "Looking unto Jesus the author and finisher of our faith; who *for the joy that was set before him endured the cross*" (emphasis added).

Not every moment in this mortal life is going to be joyful. Often, the joy is set ahead of us, just like it was for Jesus. But, like Jesus, we can choose to keep our sights on the joy set before us to endure our trials as well.

Having trials often causes us to lose sight of the Savior, and the adversary would distract us by causing us to focus on fear, doubt, and comparison. Each of these distractions has an antidote to help us focus on the joy set before us: faith, hope, and love.

Fear

In mid-November, I contracted some kind of terrible virus that left me with a rattling sound in my chest when I would breathe. I didn't feel super sick, but it was concerning to hear the wheezing, and I still had a yucky cough.

Every few weeks, I would go back into my doctor's office. I did a round of antibiotics and a round of steroid pills, followed by a steroid inhaler and a more powerful antibiotic.

After Christmas, I was subjected to a CT scan to look for a pulmonary embolism, and I was diagnosed with bronchitis and pleurisy. I was given another round of steroid pills and inhalers.

In February, I was diagnosed with asthma and given a rescue inhaler. I tried every humidifier and air purifier I could find.

In March, I was sent to do a fancy lung capacity test called a spirograph.

In early April, I received the results that my lungs were working at 55 percent of what they would expect. So if most people have a straw to breathe through, mine would be more like a coffee straw.

I have found myself spiraling into anxiety, asking myself:

"Is this going to just keep getting worse?"

"Do I need a lung transplant?"

"Will I be able to raise my children?"

"If I die, is my husband going to find a prettier wife and love her more than me?"

Cognitively, I know that "faith and fear cannot coexist. One gives way to the other."[1] I know that faith casts out fear. But many of the Lord's chosen have experienced fear, enough that "fear not" is one of the first things his messengers say. Here are a few examples:

- "Fear not, Abram" (Genesis 15:1)
- "Fear not, Daniel" (Daniel 10:12)

- "Fear not, Mary" (Luke 1:30)
- "Fear not," shepherds (Luke 2:10)
- "Fear not," Nephites (3 Nephi 22:4)
- "Fear not, little flock" (Doctrine and Covenants 35:27)

All of us experience some fear. So, if the antidote to fear is faith, how do we increase our faith to help us focus on joy?

Elder Juan Pablo Villar provided this answer: "Just as reading and learning about muscles is not enough to build muscle, reading and learning about faith without adding action is insufficient to build faith."[2]

My lungs have been weakened by a virus and will have to be built back up little by little. It is possible, but it will take a lot of hard work and consistent effort—in my case, that means hard cardio, which I hate, to improve my endurance. The answer to your health challenges may not be as simple, albeit terrible, as mine. But often, the key to regaining our faith really does boil down to consistently doing the little things.

Just as you cannot consume all of your calories on Tuesday and expect to be full and healthy for the rest of the week, you cannot expect to be spiritually healthy and full of faith if you only remember your faith on Sunday. Prayer, fasting, studying the scriptures and the words of the prophets, pondering, attending the temple, and serving others all help us get closer to Christ because we are practicing being like Him. And in doing so, we gain more faith in Him and Heavenly Father's plan.

One of my greatest fears was realized in 2016 when my three-year-old daughter Elsie died as the result of an accident at home. I remember thinking before her accident, probably much like many of you, that I could never survive something that painful. There are still occasionally days that I wonder if I can do it.

But I have come to know my Savior in my grief. I have come to trust Him. I believe Him when He says that all these things will be for my good. Focusing on Him and His promises and trusting in my covenants, I have come to feel overwhelmingly grateful that we have someone who knew and loved us in this life watching over our family, cheering for our success, and weeping with us during our trials.

We have more help than we know or see.

President Holland said, "Ask for angels to help you."[3]

President Joseph F. Smith declared, "When messengers are sent to minister to the inhabitants of this earth, they are not strangers, but from the ranks of our kindred [and] friends."[4]

When we think of the angels helping us, I hope you think of your own family members who have passed on. I think of my Elsie throwing glitter. I think of my Tongan grandparents and their humility and strength. I think of my Grampa Gene and Grama June, and I think of my great-grandma Thea. Above all, I think of Jesus Christ.

Jesus is with us, helping us fight our battles, and He is stronger than the adversary. Truly, we have no need to fear when He is with us.

Doubt

The next distraction from joy I wanted to discuss is doubt.

When my son, Steel, was two years old, I was making cookies with him when he began to cry after he saw me crack the eggs into the batter. He was so angry about it. He didn't want eggs! I promised him cookies! He was so upset, he slapped the mixer and tried to toss the whole thing off the counter.

I thought this was an interesting depiction of how doubt works in our lives.

Sometimes things happen that don't seem to make sense to us. As we wait for God to make cookies out of our lives, sometimes it seems like we've ended up in a big mess of slimy eggs. Perhaps the bitter taste of the baking soda or vanilla has entered in; yes, there is some sugar in the mix, but this is nothing like what you were expecting, and maybe you are disappointed in the results thus far. Maybe you are angry enough to cry out in frustration. Maybe you are ready to toss the whole thing off the counter.

Remember that "Doubt is an enemy of faith and joy. Just as warm ocean water is the breeding ground for hurricanes, doubt is the breeding ground for spiritual hurricanes. Just as belief is a choice, so is doubt."[5]

When we are experiencing doubts, the antidote is hope.

> And what is it that ye shall hope for? Behold I say unto you that ye shall have hope through the atonement of Christ and the power of his resurrection, to be raised unto life eternal, and this because of your faith in him according to the promise. (Moroni 7:41)

When we place our hopes on Jesus Christ and rely on His promises, it will strengthen our faith. Those two virtues tend to walk hand in hand.

How do we practice hope?

The Lord said, "For my thoughts are not your thoughts, neither are your ways my ways, saith the Lord. For as the heavens are higher than the earth, so are my ways higher than your ways, and my thoughts than your thoughts" (Isaiah 55:8–9).

I think because the Lord knows how very little we understand, He has endless patience for our doubts. God knows that we don't know all the things He knows or see all the things He sees.

In the book of Mark, there is a story about a man who brings his possessed child to be healed by Jesus. He had taken his son many times to be healed and it had never worked. Jesus told him, "If thou canst believe, all things are possible to him that believeth" (Mark 9:23).

The man answered with my favorite line about hope: "Lord, I believe; help thou mine unbelief" (Mark 9:24).

Like that man, if we can no more than *desire* to believe, that is hope. That was enough for Jesus to work the miracle. He perfects our offerings.

Sometimes, it isn't doubt in the Lord that would distract us from feeling joy, but doubt in ourselves.

I have used my social media as a way of processing my grief and expressing my faith and hope in Christ. I only post a few times a month, but I consider it my most useful tool for sharing my faith, and in times when I have been tempted to delete it completely, I have felt impressed that the Lord would be displeased with me if I chose to discard that opportunity to share messages about Him.

The anniversary of Elsie's death is always a tender day and, annually, it takes me through waves of grief. I'm generally vulnerable and transparent with how I am really feeling, and this year I wasn't feeling my best. I found myself being a little snappier and more short-tempered with my children. The emotions of the day combined with being sick just had me in a funk.

I read a few scriptures about the worth of souls, but you know how sometimes someone will get up during testimony meeting and say "I love each and every one of you" at the end? I can be a bit of a skeptic, and I often think, "But you don't know each and every one of us." I probably was not in the right mindset, so those scriptures were giving me that same vibe. Yes, I know God "loves each and every one of us," but I needed to know that He loved *me*.

So, I went and read my patriarchal blessing. As I read what *He* sees in me, I began to think, "I hope that's true." And as that thought took root, I could feel the Holy Ghost confirming it. I could feel my confidence returning as the Lord perfected my offering of just desiring to believe. He says, "Look unto me in every thought; doubt not, fear not" (Doctrine and Covenants 6:36), which leads us to my final distraction from feeling joy.

Comparison

The old cliché, "comparison is the thief of joy" really is true. When we are experiencing trials, it is a real temptation to look side to side instead of up.

This new physical trial I've been experiencing has brought out insecurities I haven't felt in a long time. I used to be a great athlete. Back in my spandex-wearing days I played college volleyball. So when my retired mother-in-law can play hours of pickleball every morning, and I can barely lift a load of laundry out of the dryer without needing to stop and catch my breath, it is easy to feel discouraged.

I do think there is a place for competitiveness, but let me share with you a little insight I learned from my dad when he coached me in volleyball: You are in competition with yourself to be better than you were yesterday. Because of this philosophy, I'm sure I was a frustrating athlete to coach because I found it completely possible to lose a game and walk away feeling great. I also found it possible to win and still feel terrible. Yes, it was a team sport, but realistically, I could only control my own performance, so that was what I was taught to measure success or failure by. This has translated well to other areas of my life as I have moved past being in peak physical condition.

Allow me to travel a little further back in my athletic career.

In junior high and high school, I also ran track. At meets, we were each other's cheerleaders. I still remember cheering for my friends as they ran their races, and they would cheer for me. We were all on the same team, even though we all competed in different events.

Have you ever considered that perhaps comparing a shot-putter against a sprinter is not a very good measuring stick for whether or not one is a good athlete? Is it possible that this is what comparing does in our lives?

Each of us has our own set of skills, strengths, and assets that help us face the challenges of our life. So perhaps someone else's skills or blessings are not an accurate measuring stick for whether we can be successful in our life. Instead of comparing and wondering why someone else gets a javelin, or a discus, maybe we could spend a little more time cheering each other on in our respective feats.

The antidote for comparison is love. When we love the Lord, we show it through our gratitude for the life He has given us. Elder Gary Sabin said in general conference, "You will never be happier than you are grateful."[6] If we struggle with comparison during our trials, one of the best places to start is with gratitude. Gratitude will show us all the things we have to be joyful about.

I do this thing that I call "horrible-izing" when I am tempted to become irritated with someone. When someone is rude to me while driving, I come up with a whole backstory for why they did it: "Oh, sad for them . . . their dog died, and they are still pretty distracted by it."

If someone cuts in front of me in line, I think something like, "This poor soul was orphaned when they were seven, and no one ever taught them any better."

While this little exercise can be silly, it helps me to be grateful even for trials that I don't have. I really believe that if we knew each other's whole stories, it would be much easier to offer grace. When we love the Lord, we naturally become more loving and understanding of others as we come to love the things He loves.

I've always loved the phrase, "a candle loses nothing by lighting another flame." The light that we share is the light of Christ. Truly there is enough for all. There is enough light, enough love, enough blessings, and enough gifts for *all* of us. We don't need to waste time comparing ourselves to each other when there is so much joy to be found right where we are.

Jesus Christ teaches us how to find joy in every circumstance because His atoning sacrifice ensures happiness as the final result for the faithful. Even when our current circumstances may be difficult, or even tragic, we can feel joy in knowing Jesus overcame the world. As you remember your Savior, Jesus Christ, and as you make covenants with Him, I trust that you will find joy set before you in every circumstance. He has promised that you will. He never breaks His promises.

NOTES

Adapted from a talk given at BYU Women's Conference.

1. Kevin W. Pearson, "Faith in the Lord, Jesus Christ," *Ensign* or *Liahona*, May 2009.
2. Juan Pablo Villar, "Exercising Our Spiritual Muscles," *Ensign* or *Liahona*, May 2019.
3. Jeffrey R. Holland, "Place No More for the Enemy of My Soul," *Ensign* or *Liahona*, May 2010.
4. *Gospel Doctrine: Sermons and Writings of Joseph F. Smith*, (1986), 435.
5. Sean Douglas, "Facing Our Spiritual Hurricanes by Believing in Christ," *Liahona*, November 2021.
6. Gary B. Sabin, "Hallmarks of Happiness," *Liahona*, November 2023.

YOU WERE MADE TO MOURN

When Mordecai perceived all that was done, Mordecai rent his clothes, and put on sackcloth with ashes, and went out into the midst of the city, and cried with a loud and a bitter cry; and came even before the king's gate: for none might enter into the king's gate clothed with sackcloth.

And in every province, whithersoever the king's commandment and his decree came, there was great mourning among the Jews, and fasting, and weeping, and wailing; and many lay in sackcloth and ashes.

So Esther's maids and her chamberlains came and told it her. Then was the queen exceedingly grieved; and she sent raiment to clothe Mordecai, and to take away his sackcloth from him: but he received it not. (Esther 4:1–4)

THROUGH THE WILDERNESS

Tammy Uzelac Hall

TAMMY UZELAC HALL is mom to four wildly fabulous daughters and wife to her favorite human, Jim Hall. She is an author and the host of the LDS Living/Deseret Bookshelf Plus podcast, *Sunday on Monday*. Her love of the scriptures grew from the years she spent as a full-time seminary and institute teacher, turning her into a lifelong student of the Hebrew language.

It was my last semester at Ricks college, and I knew that summer semester would be a breeze. As I was preparing to register for classes, my roommate jokingly said, "You should sign up for Discovery." A burst of laughter rang from my roommates, and they all made jokes about me on "Discovery." The assumption was universal: I did not have what it took to successfully complete the Discovery program.

Discovery is an intensive, five-week study abroad experience where you live in the Idaho wilderness. Lest you think I was in France sampling cheeses or in Spain eating paella, I was living off the land along the banks of the Salmon River in Idaho. We rafted to the bottom of the river and then spent five weeks hiking back to the top, all the while studying the humanities, science, history, botany, and religion. Naturally, I opted out of the religion course. My roommates' mockery fueled my pride and I resolved to register for Discovery.

The wilderness taught me a lot—toilet paper is a necessity, chocolate is a delicacy, deodorant is not optional, food is essential, and my roommates were right, I was way out of my league. But the most important lesson I learned is that God is unquestionably real. About three weeks into the program, I was profoundly hungry. We had been living off powdered eggs, beef jerky, and granola bars. This was *Survivor* before there was *Survivor*. Thankfully, one of the guys in my group brought a fishing pole, and I asked if I could borrow it. Now, for the record, I hate fish! But I was starving and I knew I needed food. I fished along the banks of the Salmon River, confident that I would catch something. But I didn't. I was there for over an hour casting out and reeling in that fishing line so, in utter desperation, I set the pole down, got on my knees and prayed.

"Heavenly Father, please help me catch a fish. I am so hungry." I have no doubt that God rolled His eyes and said, "But you hate fish, remember?" Nevertheless, I continued to ask for help. I got up and began to fish and after four or five casts, I caught a fish! It was such a glorious moment. I began jumping up and down, yelling to everyone that I had indeed caught a fish. I was so excited that the fish nearly slipped from my grasp. I was beaming. Everyone in my group ran over to see that glorious fourteen-inch trout. It wasn't much, but it was everything to me, and that night, we dined like kings. That night, I also knew that God was not only real but that He was capable of hearing my prayers . . . even in the wilderness.

What do you imagine in your mind when you hear the word *wilderness*? Close your eyes for just a moment and paint a landscape in your mind of what you imagine your wilderness looks like. What is or isn't in your wilderness?

The word *wilderness* has been a topic of study for me over the past few years. It appears many times in scripture. In fact, it's in the Bible 293 times, the Book of Mormon 252 times, the Doctrine and Covenants 17 times and the Pearl of Great Price, once. In all, the word appears roughly 563 times in scripture. Now, nearly every reference to the word *wilderness* is either going *into* the wilderness, going *through* the wilderness, or going *out* of the wilderness.

Here are some familiar examples of people in scripture who spent time in the wilderness:

- Adam and Eve (Moses 4)
- Moses and the children of Israel (Exodus 14)
- Lehi, Sariah, and family (1 Nephi 2:2 and 2 Nephi 5:6)
- Alma the Elder (Mosiah 23:1)
- Sons of Mosiah (Alma 17:7–8)
- Brother of Jared, family, and friends (Ether 2:5)
- Jesus Christ (Matthew 4:1)

Many of us are familiar with Jesus Christ's forty days and forty nights in the wilderness fasting, and for sure, He was hungry (see Matthew 4:2). Moses and the children of Israel spent forty years in the wilderness. I absolutely love the number *forty* in Hebrew because it is a symbol for "a period of test or trial; the time it takes to learn a lesson."[1] Now, *forty* could absolutely mean forty days' time, but what if it did mean the time it takes to learn a lesson? A period of test or trial? How many of us feel like we have been in our forties for a really long time? Whichever interpretation of *forty* you want to use, time was spent in the wilderness.

My Hebrew professor taught me something astounding about the word *wilderness*. In Hebrew, the word for *wilderness* is מדבר (midbar). The root for this word is דבר (dabar), which means "word." It also means "word of God, as a divine communication in the form of commandments, prophecy, and words of help to His people"[2] How amazing is that? God's help to His people can be found in the wilderness. This is true for Jesus and the children of Israel. Christ went into the wilderness: "And when he had fasted forty days and forty nights, *and had communed with God,* he was afterwards an hungered, *and was left to be tempted of the devil*" (JST Matthew 4:2). Pharoah finally let the children of Israel go, and "God led the people about, through the way of the wilderness of the Red sea" (Exodus 13:18). But before the children of Israel could meet God, they had to leave Egypt. They left familiarity to wander for forty years in search of land flowing with milk and honey otherwise known as the promised land (see Exodus 3:8). Here is what Rabbi Steven Kushner teaches about this experience and the wilderness:

> If you want to leave your Egypt and get to your Promised Land, you have to be willing to traverse wilderness. *Midbar* is a place of nothing. It is empty. There are no guarantees in wilderness, no assurances. It can be scary. It is a place of wandering (which can, at times, feel endless). But it is also a place of discovery. *Midbar*—from the root

דבר, which also is the root for "word" in Hebrew—is where Torah (God's word) is found. Wilderness is where we meet God. Wilderness is where we encounter our self. It is the place of growth. And there's no getting around it. *Midbar* is the only way to the Promised Land. It is a sacred place.[3]

Wilderness is where we meet God. A few years ago, I was talking to my friend Aliah Hall, who is a licensed therapist and is the Mental Health and Wellness Specialist for the BYU Marriot School of Business, and she added to my understanding of the word *wilderness*. I asked her, "What can we do when someone we love is having a faith crisis?" Here was her response:

"Let's reframe this idea of a faith crisis. With all the examples of people in the wilderness, it is when our Heavenly Father wants his people to grow. It's almost like He is saying: 'Hey, you over there, you need to change or grow . . . and you're going to have to pass through a wilderness.' So, I think sometimes with some of our friends and our family . . . they haven't lost their knowledge of the gospel: they are traveling through the wilderness."

This idea took me to a story about a woman in scripture who spent time in the wilderness. Her name is Hagar, and she knew the wilderness.

Abram and Sarai (whose names had not yet been changed to Abraham and Sarah) were unable to have children, but were promised by the Lord that they would. So, Sarai gave her blessing to have Abraham marry her Egyptian handmaid, Hagar. Hagar became pregnant, and this upset the balance of power between Sarai and Hagar. The scriptures tell us that Hagar's mistress Sarai was despised in Hagar's eyes (see Genesis 16:4). As a result, Sarai "dealt hardly with her" (Genesis 16:6), so Hagar left and went into the wilderness.

I imagine Hagar thinking, "This is so dumb! I don't need to be treated like this! I can go back to Egypt and live with the people who love me." There is no mention of how long Hagar was in the wilderness, but enough time had passed that, due to thirst, she ended up at a fountain of water. While she was there, an angel of the Lord appeared and asked her where she came from and where she was going. Hagar explained the situation and the angel told her to go back and submit herself to Sarai. The angel of the Lord told Hagar that if she returned, she would be blessed—presumably through the Abrahamic covenant that she married into—and that she would have a son which she was to name Ishmael. After this miraculous exchange in the wilderness, Hagar "called the name of the Lord that spake unto her, Thou God seest me: for she said, Have I also here looked after him that seeth me?" (Genesis 16:13). But I prefer the Hebrew translation of this verse: "And she called the name of the Lord who spoke to her, You are El Roi, the God who sees me."[4]

Hagar met God in the wilderness. She knew she had been seen and because of this, she is the only woman in scripture to give the Lord a name: El Roi, which means "God sees me." That fountain of water that Hagar sat by also receives a name in Genesis 16:14: "Beer-lahai-roi," which translates to, "well of the living one who sees me." I wonder how much Hagar, as an Egyptian woman, even knew about God and His ways. Hagar left her marriage and home, a place of familiarity, willing to forfeit the blessings associated with the covenant, to go into the wilderness. But it was exactly where she needed to be to have this touchstone moment with God. It has made me reflect on the moments when God saw me in the wilderness. What about your moments? When has God seen you? What are your El Roi moments, when the Living One saw you in the wilderness? Think about that for a moment: an answered (or unanswered) prayer, a feeling of peace, a change in direction, or a stupor of thought. God meets us in the wilderness.

Hagar retuned to Sarai and Abram and gave birth to Ishmael. Sarai and Abram's names were changed to Sarah and Abraham, and Sarah finally conceived. After Isaac was weaned (when he was roughly two to three years old), a festival was held.[5] Abraham invited friends and family to celebrate this milestone for his son Isaac. Around this same time, Sarah noticed an altercation between Isaac and his fourteen-year-old brother Ishmael. The scripture says Ishmael was "mocking" his brother Isaac, but some scholars believe it may have been more than mocking, which is why Sarah insisted that Ishmael and Hagar be cast out from the home.[6] This made Abraham sad, but the Lord assured him that Hagar and Ishmael would be okay and that, in fact, Ishmael would become a great nation. Abraham woke up early in the morning, took bread, a bottle of water, and gave them to Hagar and "she departed, and wandered in the wilderness" (Genesis 21:14).

As soon as their water supply ran dry, Hagar knew their fate was death. She placed her son beneath a shrub and walked away, unable to bear the burden of watching her son die. While alone, she began to weep, and the angel of God called out to her, asking her what was wrong. The angel immediately told her not to be afraid because God had heard the voice of the lad. Now, this probably didn't surprise Hagar because Ishamel in Hebrew means "God hears me." But it was what the angel said next that gave her assurance: "For God hath heard the voice of the lad *where he is*" (Genesis 21:17; emphasis added). God not only heard the lad but He heard the lad exactly *where he was*. In the wilderness.

The angel then instructed Hagar: "Arise, lift up the lad, and hold him in thine hand. . . . And God opened her eyes, and she saw a well of water; and she went, and filled the bottle with water, and gave the lad drink" (Genesis 21:18–19). I used to read this and think, "Oh, isn't it amazing that God helped her find a well?" But I think I got it wrong. She wasn't blind going into the wilderness. She could see just fine, and she was familiar with wells. So, what did God open her eyes to? That moment at the earlier well of water—*her* moment when she knew she had been seen. He was reminding her, "Hagar, it's me, El Roi. Remember? Think back to when I saw you. When I came to you in the wilderness and helped you in what seemed like a hopeless and devastating moment? Well, I'm still here, and now I am here for your son. So, lift him up, hold him, and give him something to drink."

All we need to do is remember El Roi. Our loved ones are heard and seen where they are. We need to lift them up, hold them, and remember that we too, like Hagar, are in the wilderness. Life is not made up of isolated wilderness moments—this life *is* the wilderness, and we all need God. Like the children of Israel, we couldn't stay where we were (our pre-earth life of comfort and familiarity), and we know where we want to end up, so for now, we are traversing the wilderness and meeting God over and over and over again.

Rabbi Kushner continues with his thoughts on wilderness:

> We focus so much on the things with which we struggle, we direct so much of our attention onto our hopes and dreams. Yet the place wherein we eat and sleep and argue and love, the day-to-day journeys that move us from and to and sometimes back again, the ordinary landscape of life somehow gets overshadowed. But, well we know, it is the most important part.[7]

Our heavenly parents are counting on the wilderness. They stand ready to see us, hear us, and meet us for every crucial step along the way. I have laughed many times at myself because I used to think that being single was my wilderness and that marriage would be my land flowing with milk and honey. Then I got married and it turns out that marriage and kids is the wilderness. And I have met God many times in the wilderness. But maybe you are still worried for your loved ones when it comes to covenants, church, the temple, and making good choices. Close your eyes one more time and pull up the wilderness you painted at the beginning. I want you to paint one more thing in your portrait: a ladder.

Why a ladder?

Joseph Smith taught this about a ladder:

> When you climb up a ladder, you must begin at the bottom, and ascend step by step, until you arrive at the top; and so it is with the principles of the gospel—you must begin with the first, and go on until you learn all the principles of exaltation. But it will be a great while after you have passed through the veil before you will have

learned them. It is not all to be comprehended in this world; it will be a great work to learn our salvation and exaltation even beyond the grave.[8]

So don't be afraid. Lift the people you love up. Hold them and remember the God who sees you. I will tell you this: the Idaho wilderness almost broke me. It was hot, dirty, dry, bug-infested, and in certain parts completely and totally desolate. My pack was heavy, and I was a sweaty, stinky mess . . . and I was seen in that wilderness. El Roi helped me catch that fish that day, and I have not stopped "fishing." I learned a lifetime of lessons in the Idaho wilderness and am so grateful for the experience. I think when all is said and done, we may say the same thing about our lifetime wilderness experience. The wilderness is where we are meant to be and, thankfully, it is not where we are expected to remain. The wilderness is not our permanent home, and I can't wait for the prophetic promise from Isaiah to be fulfilled: "For the Lord shall comfort Zion: he will comfort all her waste places; and he will make her wilderness like Eden, and her desert like the garden of the Lord; joy and gladness shall be found therein, thanksgiving, and the voice of melody" (Isaiah 51:3).

NOTES

Adapted from a talk given at BYU Women's Conference.

1. John J. Davis, *Biblical Numerology: A Basic Study of the Use of Numbers in the Bible* (Ada, MI: Baker Academic, 1968) 121–122. See also J. C. Cooper, *An Illustrated Encyclopaedia of Traditional Symbols* (London: Thames & Hudson, 1987) 120; E. W. Bullinger, *Number in Scripture* (Digireads.com, 2020) 266; Robert D. Johnston, *Numbers in the Bible: God's Unique Design in Biblical Numbers* (Grand Rapids, MI: Kregel

Publications, 1999) 85; Maurice H. Farbridge, *Studies in Biblical and Semitic Symbolism* (Eugene, OR: Wipf and Stock, 2007) 144–45, 155–56; Kevin J. Todeschi, *The Encyclopedia of Symbolism* (Perigee Trade, 1995) 187; and Alonzo Gaskill, "Forty," *The Lost Language of Symbolism: An Essential Guide for Recognizing and Interpreting Symbols of the Gospel* (Salt Lake City: Deseret Book, 2003).

2. Francis Brown, S. R. Driver, and Charles A. Briggs, *The Brown-Driver-Briggs Hebrew and English Lexicon* (Peabody, MA: Hendrickson, 1997), 184.
3. Steven Kushner, "Becoming Midbar," *Reform Judaism*, accessed May 23, 2024, https://reformjudaism.org/learning/torah-study/torah-commentary/becoming-midbar.
4. Robert Alter, *The Five Books of Moses: A Translation with Commentary* (New York: W. W. Norton and Company, 2004) 53.
5. See Bruce R. McConkie, *The Mortal Messiah: From Bethlehem to Calvary, Book 1* (Salt Lake City: Deseret Book, 1979) 223.
6. Andrew C. Smith, "Hagar in LDS Scripture and Thought," *The Interpreter Foundation*, August 30, 2019, https://journal.interpreterfoundation.org/hagar-in-lds-scripture-and-thought/.
7. Steven Kushner, "Becoming Midbar."
8. *Teachings of Presidents of the Church: Joseph Smith* (2007), 268.

YOU WERE MADE FOR COURAGE

[Mordecai] gave . . . the copy of the writing of the decree that was given at Shushan to destroy them, to shew it unto Esther . . . and to charge her that she should go in unto the king, to make supplication unto him, and to make request before him for her people. . . .

Again Esther spake unto . . . Mordecai;

All the king's servants, and the people of the king's provinces, do know, that whosoever, whether man or woman, shall come unto the king into the inner court, who is not called, there is one law of his to put him to death, except such to whom the king shall hold out the golden sceptre, that he may live: but I have not been called to come in unto the king these thirty days. (Esther 4:8-11)

WEBS OF FRIENDSHIP

Ardeth G. Kapp

ARDETH GREENE KAPP (1931–2024) was a native of Glenwood, Alberta, Canada, and served as the ninth general president of the Young Women Organization of The Church of Jesus Christ of Latter-day Saints. She received academic degrees from the University of Utah and Brigham Young University and was the author of twenty books.

One of my favorite books to share with children is *Charlotte's Web*, by E. B. White. Although it is a book for children, it holds great insight into the source of joy for all of us, at every age and stage. If you have read that book, you will remember that Charlotte is the spider and Wilbur the pig. Poor Wilbur: we read that on a "dreary rainy day" he felt so "friendless, dejected, and hungry [that] he threw himself down in the manure and sobbed."[1] He felt left out, ignored, not appreciated. Have you ever had a Wilbur day? A day when you felt that alone and discouraged?

Let me remind you of how Wilbur was rescued from his plight

in a way that turned sadness into joy. He was visited by Charlotte the spider, whom he hadn't liked at all when he first met her. But over the years he discovered a true friend in Charlotte, one who was willing to save his life by tirelessly spinning a beautiful web with a message that would let people know he was no ordinary pig and should not be slaughtered. Even Wilbur began to believe he was something special because his friend told him he was. "'Oh Charlotte,' he said, 'to think that when I first met you I thought you were cruel and bloodthirsty!' When he recovered from his emotion, he spoke again. 'Why did you do all this for me?' he asked. 'I don't deserve it. I've never done anything for you.'

"'You have been my friend,' replied Charlotte. 'That in itself is a tremendous thing. I wove my webs for you because I liked you. . . . By helping you, perhaps I was trying to lift up my life a trifle. Heaven knows anyone's life can stand a little of that.'"[2]

Maybe I relate to this story because I was raised on a farm with pigs and, yes, lots of spiders and spiderwebs in the barn. But it makes a great point: Anyone you encounter may be having a Wilbur day. What might happen if you took just a minute to spin, not a spiderweb, but a web of friendship by saying a warm "hi" to someone, maybe even a stranger?

We are all so ordinary, and yet each of us is special and unique. When we come to know that we are literally brothers and sisters in the same family, away from our heavenly home for a time, we begin to really recognize each other—not in relation to positions, possessions, prestige, or power, but rather heart to heart and soul to soul. And then, when we meet, we don't exchange just words—a wonderful exchange of the spirit takes place, spinning spiritual webs that lift us and build us and bind us to one another.

When we are engaged in spinning spiritual webs to lift each other, it is a joyful feeling. As the Lord tells us, "My spirit . . . shall enlighten your mind, which shall fill your soul with joy" (Doctrine and Covenants 11:13).

In the words of Edward Everett Hale, an American clergyman: "I am only one, but I am one. I cannot do everything, but I can do something; and what I can do, that I ought to do; and what I ought to do, by the grace of God I shall do."[3]

Following a women's conference in another state where I had been asked to speak, a group of approximately five hundred sisters were gathered. It appeared that everyone was enjoying the warmth and blessing of being included, being in association with sisters older and younger, richer and poorer, some with children and some without, married and single, and all in between. It appeared to be a joyous occasion for everyone. I didn't notice anyone standing alone or appearing to be left out.

Shortly after my return home, I received a card in the mail postmarked from that location but bearing no return address. The card had a large, colorful turtle on the front. Inside was a short message: "Thank you, Sister Kapp, for taking your precious time to look at me. So few people care nowadays." Which sister was she, I wondered, to whom such a small gesture as a kind look would make such a difference? I wanted to go back and talk with her and give her a hug and a word of encouragement. I wished I could spend a little time with just her alone, time to get to know and love her. If just to be looked at could be appreciated, I wondered if it were possible that there may have been other sisters in that large gathering who might have had a feeling of not being recognized or included or acknowledged or appreciated.

Is it possible that in our daily comings and goings we might lift another with a chance word, a tap on the shoulder, or just an expression that conveys a feeling of respect and love? Maybe it is that easy to communicate a message that someone cares.

In our technology-crammed, busy world, it seems everything is on fast forward, and if we are not careful, we might miss a moment when we might be helpful. We might bypass an opportunity to be an actual instrument in the Lord's hands, even an answer to someone's prayer.

In the words of C. S. Lewis:

> In Friendship . . . we think we have chosen our peers. In reality, a few years' difference in the dates of our births, a few more miles between certain houses, the choice of one university instead of another . . . the accident of a topic being raised or not raised at a first meeting—any of these chances might have kept us apart. But, for a Christian, there are, strictly speaking, no chances. A secret Master of the Ceremonies has been at work. Christ, who said to the disciples "Ye have not chosen me, but I have chosen you," can truly say to every group of Christian friends "You have not chosen one another but I have chosen you for one another." The Friendship is not a reward for our discrimination and good taste in finding one another out. It is the instrument by which God reveals to each the beauties of all the others.[4]

One day, following a kind act, someone may ask, "Why did you do that for me?" And you might simply answer, like Charlotte, "You have been my friend, and that in itself is a tremendous thing."

NOTES

Adapted from a chapter in *Doing What We Came to Do: Living a Life of Love* (Deseret Book, 2012).

1. E. B. White, *Charlotte's Web* (Harper & Brothers: New York, 1952), 30.
2. White, *Charlotte's Web,* 164.
3. As quoted in John Blaydes, comp., *The Educator's Book of Quotes (Thousand Oaks, CA: Corwin Press, 2003)* 18.
4. C. S. Lewis, *The Four Loves* (London: Geoffrey Bles, 1960), 89.

YOU WERE MADE FOR THIS MOMENT

Then Mordecai commanded to answer Esther, Think not with thyself that thou shalt escape in the king's house, more than all the Jews. For if thou altogether holdest thy peace at this time, then shall there enlargement and deliverance arise to the Jews from another place; but thou and thy father's house shall be destroyed: and who knoweth whether thou art come to the kingdom for such a time as this? (Esther 4:13–14)

JESUS CHOOSES THE UNEXPECTED AS HIS MESSENGERS

Shima Baughman

SHIMA BAUGHMAN is a public educator, author, and law professor at BYU and the Wheatley Institute. A former Fulbright scholar turned TikToker (@closertojesuschrist), Shima spreads the joy of the gospel on her social media when she is not hanging out with her five children and husband, Ryan.

I want you to close your eyes and imagine that you have the next brilliant idea that is going to change the world. Who do you want to choose to get the message out about your idea? Who do you pick as the face of your company? Think of this person. Are they tall? Charismatic? Maybe they have nice hair. Maybe they have a big following already. Are they a celebrity or athlete or musician, or someone funny? Who would you choose as your spokesperson if you could choose anyone?

Who would Jesus choose?

Jesus chose the *unexpected* to be his messengers.

Think of one of Jesus's first messengers: the Samaritan woman at the well. When Jesus met her, she was getting water during the heat of the day, not in the morning with the other women. She was a woman with five husbands over the course of her life and was living with a man she was not married to, all of which was shameful in her culture. She was an outsider in her own community, and a Samaritan—a people who were looked down upon among the Jews, so much so that the apostles were surprised Jesus wanted to even travel through this community rather than go around it. She was surprised that Jesus, a faithful Jew, would ask her for water since she would have been considered unclean. Yet Jesus came to her with compassion for her past. He knew all her sins and told her that if she would drink living water, she would never thirst. He told her that He was the Messiah, and she believed.

Jesus chose her as the first one to inform that He was the Messiah when beginning His public ministry, which is significant.[1] He chose a woman who would have been looked down upon by the general public at the time. But a key piece of this story that isn't often considered is that she also was the first to announce His ministry to the rest of her city. She was Jesus's first messenger to the broader public.

There are five key lessons for us as we consider the Samaritan woman at the well, as Christ's unexpected messenger:

1. She already believed in Jesus!

She already believed that the Messiah would come and "tell us all things" (John 4:25). Do you know enough to share with others? Do you have faith that God lives, and that Jesus Christ is our Savior? Do you believe you are a child of God? Or do you feel unqualified?

Paul was neither handsome, nor tall, nor a great orator, but he was faithful and studied and used the gifts God gave him. He was one of the greatest early missionaries, despite his past as a blasphemer.[2] Satan would try to tell you that you aren't good enough to share the gospel. That you aren't a perfect Christian. That you don't know enough. That it is too late for you to start. But if you pray, the Spirit will let you know in your heart that none of that is true. You can be a powerful witness because of your imperfections—not despite them. And you might be able to connect with some who have endured your same trials or sins and are looking for redemption from our Savior.[3]

Abish was a secret convert to the gospel of Jesus Christ and, having witnessed the miracle that Ammon performed on King Lamoni, and his Queen and all the servants in the house being incapacitated, "she ran forth from house to house, making it known unto the people" despite her status as a servant. She hoped that everyone, seeing the entire house struck down, would "cause them to believe in the power of God" (Alma 19:17).

Aren't we glad they opened their mouths, despite their limitations? Aren't we glad they were willing to preach His word and do His work? If you pray to have the Spirit with you, you can testify of what you know.

2. The Samaritan woman could not wait to testify of Him—she dropped everything and ran!

When the Samaritan woman met Jesus, it was likely hot and she needed to get water. But she only cared about sharing His important message (see John 4:28). She dropped her water pot—without hesitation— and hurried to the city. She could think of nothing she wanted to do more than to share her experience with the Savior.

Social media provides many more opportunities than our daily lives to share our testimonies and follow the admonition of our leaders to testify of Christ. Sister Bonnie Cordon tells us to "never give up an opportunity to testify of Christ."[4] I would add to Sister Cordon's brilliant insight: *You will never regret testifying of Jesus Christ.*

And, instead of at the water well, like it or not, people are spending on average two hours and twenty-three minutes a day on social media—or our modern-day water well.[5]

3. The Samaritan woman approached ALL with the good news, not just her close friends and family.

She went to the people in town and said, "Come, see . . . is not this the Christ?" Then they went out of the city and came unto Him (John 4:28–30). Are we sometimes afraid to share our testimonies more broadly than with our inner circles?

I am so grateful for the valiance of one particular woman who was willing to share the gospel beyond her immediate circle because it changed my life. Her name is Maryam. She was a nurse at UCLA Medical Center and a Persian convert to the Church. At work one day, she saw a new immigrant from Iran. He spoke broken English with a huge accent. She had the prompting to talk to him about the gospel. But she was afraid. She thought, "He is Muslim, he will not want to hear about Jesus Christ." The prompting came again, and she dismissed it, deciding in her mind that it was not safe to talk to him about the gospel as there are severe penalties for converting from Islam to Christianity. Then she saw him again at a water fountain. The prompting came a third time. She could not deny the prompting this time. She went up to him and invited him and his family to her Christmas party. He quickly said yes. This man at the water fountain was my father, and because Maryam was not afraid to open her mouth, my family had the opportunity to become members of The Church of Jesus Christ of Latter-day Saints, which brought miracles that changed the course of the future of my family for good.

4. The Samaritan woman bore personal testimony of what Jesus did for her and let them come to their own conclusion.[6]

The Samaritan woman said, "He told me all things that ever I did. Is not this the Christ?" (John 4:28–29). This is what we do with the gospel. We share our experience with our Savior and let people choose for themselves and come to their conclusion that Jesus Christ is their personal Savior. The pattern was set beautifully by the Savior's first messenger to the public.

As a result of the brave Samaritan woman's influence, "many of the Samaritans of that city believed on him," and they asked Jesus to stay with them (John 4:39). He stayed two days to teach the others! And *then* they came to their own testimony: "And said unto the woman, Now we believe, not because of thy saying: for we have heard him ourselves, and know that this is indeed the Christ, the Saviour of the world" (John 4:42).

Jesus chose an unexpected woman to be his messenger. And

she happened to be perfect for the job. This happens today: when you share the gospel on social media, joy multiplies.

Here is an example of this:

Ashli Carnicelli is an Italian opera singer who grew up Catholic and found the Church at the age of thirty-five.[7] She was influenced by a member of the Church who was a fashion blogger. She says, "It wasn't just the way her home was decorated or her style of dress that drew me to learn more about this special Church she belonged to—it was that her light shined so brightly and so visibly, like a beacon . . . I wanted to be like her too!" Since converting to the Church, she has used her social media to spiritually influence others as well. Goodness was multiplied by two women willing to share their light.

5. The Samaritan woman was vulnerable with her struggles and her joy.

The woman at the well went from being ashamed to be with others to being an influencer among them. She was getting water during the heat of the day, rather than in the morning with the other women, because of her past sins and likely negative reputation, but those things no longer mattered once she found her Savior Jesus Christ. She stopped worrying about how she would be perceived and what she lacked. She put all thoughts of herself aside and went to tell everyone about Him.

Sharing the gospel doesn't have to be all roses and rainbows—you can also share how Jesus Christ helps you in your most difficult moments. The experts teach us we should be vulnerable with our testimonies and experiences in gaining faith.[8]

For instance, Shannon tragically lost her baby boy in 2021,

and sharing her testimony of her Savior has helped her answer others' prayers.[9] Jonathan shares that while going through a divorce, he started an account that helped him show his children the gospel He knew when they were away from him.[10]

Could Jesus use some messengers today? Could *you* be one of His messengers?

I would like to share my story of going from being a social media hater to sharing goodness online on TikTok and Instagram.

I had this profound realization when the world shut down during the pandemic that the Lord's work was hastening. I started evaluating my life. Was I giving all I could to build the kingdom of God on earth? I knew that I wasn't.

I had been a law professor for thirteen years, writing and researching about criminal justice policy, but I realized that no amount of policy was ever going to change someone's life. I saw that policy was temporary, changed at the whim of a new legislature, but hearts could change through conversion to the gospel. I saw people give up drugs through finding Jesus Christ. I saw judges who ignored empirical data but exercised mercy in setting lower bail amounts when a defendant's ministering brothers and sisters attended court with them. I realized that no amount of policy would redeem a soul. Jesus Christ is the answer to all our world's problems, our social ills, and our personal tribulations.[11]

I felt called to do more to spread the gospel of Jesus Christ. I prayed to ask Heavenly Father what I should do. Before long, I felt compelled by the Spirit to get on social media and talk about the good that Jesus Christ does in our lives. I wanted to unify Christians and share light, particularly to young people who have been leaving religion. But I was so scared! My world up to this point was academia. Academics get paid for being critical about everything. To go public with my faith and share with people I didn't know, I had to overcome a lot of pride and fear of what people would think of me. I don't think the world of academia is too different from your world or your social circles.

But . . . Jesus uses the unexpected to share His message!

So, in 2022, I got on TikTok and started making videos telling people of God's love for them and sharing insights I gained from scriptures. I soon started sharing on Instagram too.

It still isn't something I feel like I am good at, but I have a unique voice—as do you—and I know every voice allows the Spirit to touch a different heart. As Paul teaches us, we are the body of the Church and the body of Christ. And the body doesn't need only eyes or feet or hands, it needs all the parts. All of us. And our unique voices. (See 1 Corinthians 12:12–27).

An unexpected blessing of sharing the gospel online is that you can find a community of disciples of Christ on social media. I have learned a lot from the passion, depth of faith, and openness of Christians sharing their testimonies. I used to feel that it was rude to talk openly about your faith or pray in mixed company; now, I feel blessed to do it. We can be respectful of nonbelievers and people of other faiths while still feeling joy in our testimonies.

Social media use should certainly still come with some warnings. In general, if you spend any time on social media, it is better to be posting positive uplifting content or commenting than just consuming—even if you just repost what you like from others! Your friends might not have seen it or might need to see it. Studies show that people who use social media actively (rather than passively) are often happier with their use of it.[12]

It is not easy to be on social media and keep thinking celestial. Remind yourself constantly that your singular focus is bringing people to Jesus Christ. If you only have time to study the word of God or use social media, your personal scripture study must come first! And once you read it, you may want to screenshot it and share it with your friends!

Want to hear my final pitch? Well, it's actually Jesus's final pitch. What was the last thing Jesus told His apostles in Jerusalem? The final message of Jesus Christ that the apostles wanted us to know?

In the last part of Matthew, Jesus says, "Go ye therefore, and teach all nations, baptizing them in the name of the Father, and of the Son, and of the Holy Ghost" (Matthew 28:19). Mark 16:15 says, "And he said unto them, go ye into all the world and preach the gospel to every creature." And in the final chapter of Luke, Jesus told His apostles that "repentance and remission of sins should be preached in His name among all nations beginning at Jerusalem" (Luke 24:47).

And, of course, famously, in the final chapter of John, Jesus said, *Lovest thou me? Feed my lambs. Feed my sheep. Feed my sheep* (see John 21:15–17).

A careful study of the New Testament will tell you that there are few acts recorded in all four gospels. The Great Commandments are only in three of the gospels.[13] No parables are listed in all four gospels. But there is *one* message the apostles all share with us: *share His word. Share His truth.* Testify of the miracles he has performed for us. Testify of His power in our lives.

To women in the Church, our Prophet today and President Hinckley have both echoed President Spencer W. Kimball's prophetic words that "much of the major growth that is coming to the Church in the last days will come because many of the good women of the world . . . will be drawn to the Church in large numbers. This will happen to the degree that the women of the Church reflect righteousness and articulateness in their lives and to the degree that the women of the Church are seen as distinct and different—in happy ways—from the women of the world."[14]

How are you happier in having found the gospel of Jesus Christ? How has the gospel of Jesus Christ changed your life? You are uniquely situated—with your personality, your skills, your life experience, your unique testimony—to be a messenger of the gospel to reach unique individuals *only you* can reach.

Maryam was one of the few Persian-speaking members of the Church in all of UCLA, and she invited my father to come celebrate Christ. It had to be her.

Jesus Christ uses the unexpected to be His messengers. I choose to be one of His unexpected messengers. He has saved me from death. He lifts me from daily sin. He succors me in my times of need and heals me. I pray that we will build His Kingdom together, and show the world the happiness only He can bring.

NOTES

Adapted from a talk given at BYU Women's Conference.

1. In John 4:25, the Samaritan woman says, "I know that Messias cometh, which is called Christ: when he is come, he will tell us all things." And "Jesus saith unto her, I that speak unto thee am he" (John 4:26). Note that Jesus had hinted to Nicodemus of His status as the Messiah (see

John 3:2–5), and Peter had also recognized that He was "the Christ" in response to a question (Matthew 16:16).
2. Before Paul became a missionary, he says he was a "blasphemer, and a persecutor and injurious: *but I obtain mercy*" (1 Timothy 2:13; emphasis added).
3. Moses and Joseph Smith also felt unqualified. They felt they were too weak at public speaking to be God's prophets, but they were both critical to building His kingdom. Moses saved God's people from slavery, parted the Red Sea, delivered the Ten Commandments, and brought his people a tabernacle to worship God. Joseph Smith translated the Book of Mormon, built the first modern-day temples, and restored the priesthood keys and sealing power, which has converted millions to the gospel of Jesus Christ.
4. Bonnie H. Cordon, "Never Give Up an Opportunity to Testify of Christ," *Liahona*, May 2023.
5. DataReportal, 31 January 2024, https://datareportal.com/reports/digital-2024-deep-dive-the-time-we-spend-on-social-media#:~:text=Meanwhile%2C%20analysis%20from%20data.ai,category%20rather%20than%20social%20media.
6. President Nelson has advised us that we can surprise our friends' doubting hearts with our believing hearts: "Let your skeptical friends see how much you love the Lord and His gospel. Surprise their doubting hearts with your believing heart." (Russell M. Nelson, "Choices for Eternity," Worldwide Devotional for Young Adults, May 2022).
7. Ashli Carnicelli, @ashlicarnicelli.
8. Some of the best advice I have received is from Angie Boyle King, @angieboylekind, an expert who has worked in social media for over twenty years. 1) Engage people in a positive way. 2) Make it personal—don't be afraid to be vulnerable about your struggles, though you can keep it vague for privacy. 3) Meet people where they are!
9. Shannon Jones, @theworthofsouls.
10. Jonathan Jensen, @takemoderncourage.
11. See Russell M. Nelson, "The Answer Is Always Jesus Christ," *Liahona*, May 2023.
12. Rebecca Godard & Susan Holtzman, "Are active and passive social

media use related to mental health, wellbeing, and social support outcomes? A meta-analysis of 141 studies," *Journal of Computer-Mediated Communication*, 29 (2024), https://doi.org/10.1093/jcmc/zmad055.
13. I am by no means suggesting that sharing the gospel is superior in any sort of commandment hierarchy to loving God, keeping the commandments, or loving our neighbors. I just point this out to say that sharing the gospel might be more important to our role as disciples of Christ than many of us might think.
14. Spencer W. Kimball, "The Role of Righteous Women," *Ensign*, November 1979. Both President Hinckley and President Nelson reiterated this promise and calling.

YOU WERE MADE FOR COMMUNITY

Then Esther bade them return Mordecai this answer, Go, gather together all the Jews that are present in Shushan, and fast ye for me, and neither eat nor drink three days, night or day: I also and my maidens will fast likewise; and so will I go in unto the king, which is not according to the law: and if I perish, I perish.

So Mordecai went his way, and did according to all that Esther had commanded him. (Esther 4:15-17)

BELIEVING AND BELONGING IN A BIG, BROKEN WORLD

Melissa Inouye

MELISSA WEI-TSING INOUYE (1979–2024) was a scholar of modern Chinese history and religion with AB and PhD degrees from Harvard University. She authored many books, including *Crossings: a bald Asian American Latter-day Saint woman scholar's ventures through life, death, motherhood, and cancer (not necessarily in that order)* and *Sacred Struggle: Seeking Christ on the Path of Most Resistance*.

Because of my role as a Latter-day Saint scholar, sometimes people reach out to me with questions and issues they're struggling with. They use phrases like "my shelf broke" and "it all came crashing down" and "I don't know how to make sense of this." I've observed that people who have crises of faith often express certain assumptions about what the Church is, or what it should be, which I used to share. But now my view is different.

First: as a child, I used to think that because the Restoration was all about fixing errors, our Church was error-free. But then I learned that we, the Latter-day Saints, are not immune to errors, bad judgment, social pressures, and sin. So often, we make mistakes, just like any other group of God's children. We are subject to the forces of culture and the transformations of time. We have good apples and bad apples.

Second: as a child, I used to think my Church was "the same" wherever you went. Anywhere you went in the world, there on Sunday you would find the Latter-day Saints singing the hymns of Zion and partaking of the sacrament. But then, as I lived and served in the Church in various parts of the world, I came to understand the power of culture to shape our assumptions about what the world is and how people should live in it. Even when Church members draw on the same compendium of teachings and scriptures, in our practices and interpretations—even within the same country or same neighborhood!—we can have extremely divergent beliefs and lifestyles. I realized that we, the Latter-day Saints, are incredibly different from each other.

So if we are not "error-free" and not "the same wherever you go," then what are we?

This is what I think: My Church is true *and living*. The Latter-day Saints are true *and living*. Our shared work of Zion is vital.

Error-Free?

When I was growing up in Southern California, I did kind of think the Church was the world's most perfect human organization, a place where we always knew and did only what was right. I felt we were a refuge from the world's problems.

I now see that it was completely natural for me to believe this as a child, because I grew up within a Latter-day Saint community full of amazing, Christlike people who knew me well and cared about me. I felt deeply loved and accepted. But as a young adult, as I began to observe the Church and the world more widely, I found that the Church wasn't a place of refuge for everyone.

To be clear, all large organizations, including most large religions, also struggle with prejudice, ignorance, and abuse of power. But as a university student I was troubled to learn of times in the past and in the present, as Elder Uchtdorf has said, "when members or leaders in the Church have simply made mistakes. There may have been things said or done that were not in harmony with our values, principles, or doctrine."[1] I thought: *If God is leading us, how can we make mistakes? If Jesus is here, among us, how can He allow us to inflict such harm on His sheep?* I felt like my testimony was a bit like that game with wooden blocks, Jenga, where you build a tower of blocks all stacked on one another. You take turns taking out the blocks one by one, and it becomes more and more precarious.

Over time, however, I began to see: maybe my building-block paradigm was wrong. The Church isn't a static, uniform structure. The Church is not a thing. It is people. Metaphors like "a keystone bridge" or "a shelf" or something that "comes crashing down" are evocative, but they are limited in their ability to describe the dynamic, living elements of our religious movement and of religious faith itself, which so often exists in the context of deep relationships. When we talk about "the Church" we are not describing brick and mortar, but a network of living, agentive beings, interacting with their environment and with each other over time.

As a historian, I've learned there's a certain liability in large-scale endeavors. The bigger the institution, the more people are a part of your project, and the more people are a part of your project, the more complicated and unwieldy everything becomes. Looking at the Church as an institution, we see that it has over two dozen departments staffed with directors, managers, and all sorts of minor bureaucrats (including me). There's a lot of room for humanness in a large bureaucracy. There's a lot of culture that we pick up wherever in the world we go.

This helps me to understand why recent Church leaders from President Nelson to President Oaks have been so vocal and specific in their calls to the Latter-day Saints to abandon attitudes and actions of prejudice and root out racism.[2] In October 2022, Elder D. Todd Christofferson specifically mentioned the Church as a place where we had work to do: "We should be diligent in rooting prejudice and discrimination out of the Church, out of our homes, and, most of all, out of our hearts. As our Church population grows ever more diverse, our welcome must grow ever more spontaneous and warm. We need one another."[3] These calls from our leaders could not be more clear. Of course we aren't perfect. As a people, we all have work. We are all enlisted.

So, instead of being a refuge from human problems, I have come to see our Church as a sort of central problem hub, connecting us to all the afflictions of humanity. Like every other large human organization, do we, the Latter-day Saints, have problems with sexism, racism, and nationalism? Absolutely. Do we, the Latter-day Saints, have diabetes, cancer, malaria, and AIDS? Absolutely. Do we, the Latter-day Saints, find in our own ranks the problems of poverty and malnutrition? of materialism and greed? Yes, we do.

This might sound very grim to you. But over time it has started to seem better and better to me. I don't think the purpose of life is to live problem-free. I think the purpose of life is to learn to love as God loves, and see as God sees. According to 1 John 4:20–21:

> If a man say, I love God, and hateth his brother, he is a liar: for he that loveth not his brother whom he hath seen, how can he love God whom he hath not seen? And this commandment have we from him, That he who loveth God love his brother also.

Even though most of us haven't seen God, from a certain point of view it's quite easy for us to love God. God is all-knowing and all-powerful, embodies all virtues and all goodness, loves us, etc. By contrast, humans are flawed, weak, easily deceived, and easily baited into posting horrible comments on the internet. It's quite easy for us to hate other people.

What kind of love is God's kind of love for us? Is it a kind of awed gratitude and admiration for all-powerful, all-knowing, perfect beings? Or is it a gritty, resilient commitment to and care for flawed and fallible individuals? I suspect it is the latter. To implement godly virtues, then, is to spend less time admiring God and more time learning to deal with difficult people. In a sense, when God commands, "Anyone who loves me must also love their brother and sister," it sounds kind of like a parent saying, "Anyone who wants a popsicle has to eat all their broccoli and kale." Like eating broccoli and kale, which can be tough and bitter because they're packed with fiber and nutrients, loving fellow beings who are flawed and fallible is healthy for our spiritual development. So, if God wants us to learn to love the people we see around us, we need to find ways to see a lot of people.

If there's anything one can say about Latter-day Saints, it's that they see each other a lot—at worship, at play, on missions, during conference, in temples, on Zoom devotionals . . . What better way to live in relationship with those brothers and sisters Christ acknowledged could be really difficult to love? What better venue for seeing and connecting with our fellow beings? For coming to understand how their needs differ from our own?

So, my Church is not problem-free. It is problem-full, in the sense that all the problems of humanity can be found here, in our little microcosm. But if life is not about avoiding problems, but instead, learning how to identify them and respond to them creatively and collectively, what better place to do it than here, among many sisters and brothers I would not otherwise see?

The Same Everywhere?

The second thing I used to think about the Church is that it was the same everywhere you went. I assumed the cultural forms with which I grew up were the norm all around the world.

I remember being touched, as a young person, to encounter the Church in different places and to think that despite many differences, we all believed the same things. As a sixteen-year-old in Nuremberg, Germany, I found my way to the local Latter-day Saint ward. There were the local members, a couple of American missionaries, and the familiar hymn tunes. As a university student studying abroad in Beijing, I found the small group of foreigners who met in a room in the Kunlun Hotel. When passing through Mongolia, I boarded with a local member family. In all these places I met people from many walks of life, all coming together to sing, pray, and nourish each other physically and spiritually.

Then I began to study language and culture more deeply and to learn how people's fundamental assumptions could be so different. I served a Chinese-speaking mission and later began a PhD program at Harvard in East Asian Languages and Civilizations. For instance, I learned that in Chinese, there is no male or female pronoun for God. Chinese speakers, including Latter-day Saints, never call God or "Heavenly Father" "he." There is a "godly" pronoun for God, 祂, *ta*, which sounds the same as the pronoun for males, 他, *ta*, and the same as the pronoun for females, 她, *ta*. It's just written differently. I delved into Buddhist and Confucian and Daoist texts and found completely different assumptions about the nature of reality and the nature of humanity. Even a question like "What is the purpose of life?" didn't really make sense in certain cultural contexts.

When I took a position at the University of Auckland, I encountered Māori culture. In my first semester, I horrified my students when I suggested that they sit on the tables in our lecture hall in the Māori studies building. In a Māori cultural context, sitting on a table is one of the worst things you can do. I, in turn, was horrified to realize that I could commit a rude, dishonorable deed without even knowing it.

Culture is a minefield! The invisible signs we make to each other, the honor we give or destroy by the order in which we do things, the key words and phrases that signal certain group alliances—how complex and tricky it all is!

Even aspects of Latter-day Saint life that many might feel are standard practice may vary. In some remote villages, Latter-day Saints have used bits of banana for the sacrament. When I lived in Asia in 2013, Filipina and Indonesian domestic worker branches were staffed by female ward mission leaders, female Sunday School presidents, and female ward clerks. Depending on where you are in the world, your Sabbath day may be Tuesday, Wednesday, Thursday, Friday, or Saturday.

Thus despite our tight global organization, correlated lesson manuals, and ethos of unity, it is hard to say with a great deal of specificity and certainty who exactly Latter-day Saints are, what they believe, and what they stand for in a given neighborhood or region of the world. How wide are the distances between us! We can all recite the same articles of faith, but what about when someone in a given place perceives tension between "obeying, honoring, and sustaining the law" and "being honest, true, chaste, benevolent, virtuous and doing good to all"? We can all read the same Bible and Book of Mormon in which Jesus says to do unto others as you would have them do unto you. But so often when someone says, "You're not treating me right," another says, "That's because you don't understand what's really good for you, but I do." We can all sing, "Now let us rejoice in the day of salvation. No longer as strangers on earth need we roam,"[4] but so often we cannot bear to spend even ten minutes hearing the political views or emotional pain of a fellow Latter-day Saint who seems alien to us.

With such different understandings of how the gospel of Jesus

Christ should unfold in everyday life, in a local political and cultural context, what holds us together?

Although we may have different understandings and hopes for the various rites, ordinances, manuals, and lessons we share, what holds us together is a dual vertical and horizontal orientation in our shared covenants. The baptismal covenant set out in Mosiah 18:8–10 is not only to take Christ's name upon us, but also to be one people, to bear one another's burdens and mourn with those that mourn. The temple covenants are not only to obey God and keep God's commandments but also to consecrate our time and talents to building Zion on the face of the earth. We may not understand each other, but we are fundamentally oriented toward each other as we seek God—not just turning our faces up to the heavens but also beholding each other across the world's wide divides. This horizontal orientation finds expression not only in our theology but also in our organization at the grass roots, in people-to-people networks and connections cultivated not only locally but all over the world.

Real, True, Zion

So, in sum, I don't see the Church as a place of perfection, and I don't see the Church as a place that's the same everywhere you go. We are both too small and too big for perfection and homogeneity.

The Latter-day Saints as a whole are also too real (too true, too living) for perfection and homogeneity, the values driving much of the division and polarization in society today. Both perfection and homogeneity stem from a purity mindset. "I will associate only with those who are virtuous just like me and will shun those who do not meet my high comprehensive standards, who fail my litmus tests." The problem is, the more we self-select into communities of people just like us, the more atomized and siloed our lives become. We enter echo chambers and know that this is a safe space for self-congratulation. My Uncle Charles, a scholar at Tufts University, characterized this human tendency perfectly:

> Not knowing God's gentle commands, I would seek association with those who share my values and experiences. I would avoid all others. As a result, my life would steadily become narrower and more impoverished. I would slowly lose real human interaction and understanding God loves us, so. . . [He] hands us a rake and asks us to get this and that job done.[5]

This "rake" of which Uncle Charles speaks is God's commandment to love one another as we would have others love us, and as Jesus did love everyone. Raking is hard and sometimes tedious work. Most importantly, it is not theoretical work. It requires sweaty effort, exposure to the elements and to smells of rot and fungus, and consistent effort. But the times when we obediently do this hard work of raking are the times when we turn around and see Christ, right there next to us, His own tool in hand.

When we rake in the context of the Church, we also bump elbows and scrape tines with people who are really different from us. This is, in fact, ideal. What the current moment needs instead of purity culture is exposure culture, a community that contains, by design, the full spectrum of messy human realities and fiercely claims each child of God as a beloved and indispensable family member. Only within a community that contains all of humanity, including all the difficult things about humanity, can one truly live up to the ethical demands of being human. The global Church is just such an exposure community.

So what is my Church, to me?

To me, the Church is true and living. By living, I mostly mean, the Church is *real*. This is a big deal. You may say, literally everything in the universe is real, from the gum on the bottom of my shoe to the planet Mars. This is correct. But, the point is, the Church is not simply an ideal, nor a program for proclaiming ideals. It is enacted, experienced. It is expanding and evolving. As a scholar I've spent a lot of time studying moral ideological movements. Everyone is always trying to spearhead the triumph of good over evil. Everyone wants to design a new, good society where the wrong fails and the right prevails.

And yet the bigger and grander this vision is in principle, the worse things usually work out in their implementation. It's one thing to declare righteous doctrines and behaviors and prescribe them for others. But it's another thing—a harder thing, and a more godly thing— to *be* good and loving to those who are hard to love. Cultivating Christlike virtues is not a theoretical project. The only thing that works is practice. The Church is a real place to do real work on being real children of God.

Our Latter-day Saint organizations are like a big sandbox, in two senses: First, Church is a space for interactive play, where we learn how to share, to tunnel and create with others, to learn how to not throw sand that gets in people's eyes.

Second, our Latter-day Saint organizations at all levels can be sources of persistent frustrations that not only train but transform us. The Church is, perhaps, like a rock tumbler, a container for polishing rough rocks so the colors and veins within shine. You drop rough rocks into the container, along with some sand or some other kind of grit. You turn the machine on. Over a long period of time it constantly turns and tumbles the rocks so they bump against each other and polish each other. Bits break off from one rock and become grit that helps polish others. The beautiful striations from within the rock emerge.

Such a sandbox is a tricky place to be a single-issue voter.

It is an uncomfortable spot for someone who is devoted to a single political party's platform.

It is frustrating for someone who champions a single high-minded cause.

I point this out not because I am trying to discourage us from being engaged citizens, or passionate civic activists, or people who reach out to those in need. What I am trying to say is, in our giant worldwide sandbox, all of our actions tend to bump up against each other. I wouldn't say our actions collectively cancel each other out, but we the Latter-day Saints are so diverse, and the law of agency so often mirrors the law of entropy, that even when we are trying to act together, we often get in each other's way. This can be very frustrating when one is trying to make progress in one direction only to find oneself stymied by Latter-day Saints trying to make progress in the opposite direction.

It helps me to think that the purpose of life is not to achieve the triumph of a single -ism, for these -isms vary widely with time and place. The purpose of life is to assist the Lord of the vineyard, to help the children of God flourish wherever they are planted. It's interesting to me that in Jacob's allegory of the vineyard, he went beyond the image of God's children as plants. We are both the trees and also the workers. What is important, perhaps, is not the particular -ism for which we are working, but the effort we put forth in the service of others.

By divine design, God's children are not all alike, and we disagree deeply about what is good and true. The Church is not a "solution" for the "problem" of diversity, but a preserve within which to practice it. In this our teacher is the Holy One who showed love to people most others found hard to like because they were really (and sometimes offensively) different from the norm. He taught people in their own lands and languages, amidst their own sets of cultural difficulties. His was always the path of most resistance.

This path of most resistance is the path to becoming as God now is. Seeking to return to our heavenly parents, becoming one family, covenanting with one another, becoming *as They are* through the Atonement of Christ, is the work of Zion—a task that, amidst all the Christianities and all the religious traditions with which God has blessed the people of the earth, is the collective dream and mission of the Latter-day Saints alone. Practicing unity and forbearance within our own global covenant community, exposed to humankind's full range of potential and liabilities, histories and futures, will give us the tools and experience we need to help all of God's children to flourish. We will labor in God's vineyard, humbly seeking inspiration as we tackle the world's biggest problems, until all the earth is blessed.

NOTES

Adapted from a chapter in *Sacred Struggle: Seeking Christ on the Path of Most Resistance* (Deseret Book, 2023).

1. Dieter F. Uchtdorf, "Come, Join with Us," *Ensign*, November 2013.
2. Russell M. Nelson, "Let God Prevail," *Ensign*, November 2020; Dallin H. Oaks, "Racism and Other Challenges" (Brigham Young University devotional), 27 October 2020, speeches.byu.edu.
3. D. Todd Christofferson, "The Doctrine of Belonging," *Liahona*, November 2022.
4. "Now Let Us Rejoice," *Hymns*, no. 3.
5. Charles Shirō Inouye, *Zion Earth Zen Sky: A Memoir by Charles Shirō Inouye* (Salt Lake City: Deseret Book and the BYU Maxwell Institute, 2021), 124–25.

YOU WERE MADE FOR MIGHTY THINGS

And it was so, when the king saw Esther the queen standing in the court, that she obtained favour in his sight: and the king held out to Esther the golden sceptre that was in his hand. So Esther drew near, and touched the top of the sceptre.

Then said the king unto her, What wilt thou, queen Esther? and what is thy request? it shall be even given thee to the half of the kingdom. (Esther 5:2-3)

UNITING FAMILIES THROUGH TEMPLE WORK

Jihae Kwon

JIHAE KWON was born and raised in Seoul, Korea. Her family joined the Church when she was a baby. She has studied and worked in the field of art and design for over twenty years and is currently a professor in the Fine Arts department at Brigham Young University–Hawaii.

Introduction

My all-time favorite talk is by Elder John H. Groberg, "The Power of God's Love." Elder Groberg said, "What is it about true love that touches every heart? Why does the simple phrase 'I love you' evoke such universal joy? Men give various reasons, but the real reason is that every person who comes to earth is a spirit son or daughter of God. Since all love emanates from God, we are born with the capacity and the desire to love and to be loved."[1]

Love is something we are born with. It is a divine characteristic to love and divine desire to be loved. This divine love moves

Heavenly Father and Jesus Christ to do all they have done, do, and will do for us. They are love. It is this divine love that we respond to, are motivated by, and that moves us.

In 1 Nephi 8, after partaking of the tree's fruit, Lehi wanted his family to partake of it too. This was because the tree represented "the love of God, which sheddeth itself abroad in the hearts of the children of men; wherefore, it is the most desirable above all things . . . the most joyous to the soul" (1 Nephi 11:22–23). Through that love of God, my family was brought to the true Church of Jesus Christ and now we have the gospel in our lives. His love inspires our decisions and guides our actions since joining the Church, as we try to align ourselves to Heavenly Father's plan, especially in doing genealogy work.

Three Deaths and a Birth

It took three deaths and a birth for the gospel to be introduced to my family. In November 1972, my maternal great-grandmother passed away. Exactly one year later, in November 1973, my maternal grandfather passed away. In January 1974, I was born. In February 1974, eight days after my birth, my dad passed away. My mom lost three people she loved in less than two years.

The same year in April 1974, on a Friday night before Easter, my dad, who was not religious, appeared in my mom's dream and told her about resurrection. On the following Sunday, my mom went to a church with a neighbor for the first time in her life.

Three months later, in July 1974, my mom's youngest sister, Aunt Kee Hong, walked into The Church of Jesus Christ of Latter-day Saints and asked to be baptized. A month later, in August 1974, she was baptized.

Our house was full of women, including my maternal grandmother, mom, Aunt Kee Hong, my sister, and myself. After being baptized, my aunt wanted to convert my mom because my aunt loved the gospel, and, if my mom joined the Church, it would make my aunt's life as a member of the Church much easier. My mom had a tendency to read whatever was in front of her, so my aunt started leaving Church pamphlets and the Book of Mormon around the house. One day, after reading a pamphlet about the plan of salvation, my mom was touched by the Spirit. She was baptized in November 1974.

After the two daughters' baptisms, missionaries started coming to our house to teach Grandma. The missionaries' Korean was not good, and Grandma couldn't understand many of the things they said. They spoke of Jesus Christ, Joseph Smith, Nephi, and Lehi. All these foreign names were strange and hard to remember for someone who spoke no English and was a staunch Buddhist. Grandma wanted the missionaries to stop coming. My aunt told Grandma there was only one way to stop missionaries from coming: get baptized. Then, one night, my mom's other sister, Aunt Soo Hong, saw Grandpa (a Buddhist who had only wanted one religion in his household) in her dream. He appeared, holding the Bible and heading to church, and said, "The Church of Jesus Christ of Latter-day Saints is the only true church on earth." After hearing the dream, my grandma decided to be baptized in November 1975, three years after my great-grandma's death, two years after my grandpa's death, and a year after my mom's baptism. Her niece was also baptized on the same day. Four years later, Aunt Soo Hong was baptized. It was the love of God that brought five baptisms to my family.

Patriarchal Blessing

The newly converted women in the family did their best to learn the ways of gospel living. A year after baptism, Aunt Kee Hong and my mom learned about the patriarchal blessing and decided to receive it. With their permission, I share that both their blessings talk about sharing the gospel with relatives. My aunt's blessing particularly mentions doing genealogy work. My aunt hated genealogy work because of my grandpa, who devoted many years of his life to gathering information and publishing genealogy books with his own money, which had a negative impact on his children. That was why seeing something about genealogy in Aunt Kee Hong's patriarchal blessing was displeasing. She wanted to ignore it.

Genealogy Trip

However, she decided to do something about the nagging feeling. Thirteen days after receiving the blessing, she decided to go on a genealogy trip for a week in August 1975.

My aunt saw many miracles during the trip. For example, she had to go to an island, Ulleungdo, to see relatives there. It was an eleven-hour boat ride, and she always had seasickness, so she was very worried. Thirty minutes into the ride, she was miserable. Then she passed out for eleven hours—the sound of the arrival horn woke her up. It was because of the mercy of God that she had a peaceful journey.

She didn't have the address or telephone numbers of the people she wanted to see. However, during the trip, she got off the bus exactly where she needed to, although there was no bus stop, and she turned onto the exact street she needed to without having to walk too far during the hottest time in Korea. She found houses without having a street name or house number. Before leaving on the trip, my aunt made a list of people to see and when to see them. She didn't tell any of them she was coming to see them, but she saw everybody she planned to. During the trip, she gathered all the information she needed, even the names of people who died as infants. She then submitted those names to the Church headquarters for temple ordinances to be performed.

Three years later, in 1978, my great-grandma appeared in my mom's dream. She kept saying, "Thank you, thank you." The next day, my mom received a fat envelope from Salt Lake City notifying her that the temple work for all the names Aunt Kee Hong submitted was finished, including my great-grandma's.

Although my mom and Aunt Kee Hong were not keen on genealogy work, why did they do it? Elder Benjamin De Hoyas of the Seventy shares that "the Lord encourages us as members of His Church to preserve our own family history, to learn from our ancestors, and to make the necessary arrangements for them to receive the ordinances of the gospel in the temples, to help them to progress along the covenant path, which will bless them with an eternal family. That is a central focus of the plan of our Heavenly Father: uniting family for this life and for eternity. . . . As we follow the guidance of the prophets and learn how to do our family history and perform the temple ordinances for our ancestors, we will experience great joy to the point that we will not want to stop doing it. The Spirit will flood our hearts, awaken our faculties to do it, and guide us as we search for the names of our ancestors."[2]

Temple

We learn in Isaiah 4:6 that the temple is "a tabernacle for a shadow in the daytime from the heat, and for a place of refuge, and for a covert from storm and from rain." We can rest all our worries and troubles in the temple and be embraced by God's love, mercy, and peace. It symbolizes the ultimate love and mercy of God and His Son, Jesus Christ.

President Russell M. Nelson said, "The temple lies at the center of strengthening our faith and spiritual fortitude because the Savior and His doctrine are the very heart of the temple. Everything taught in the temple, through instruction and through the Spirit, increases our understanding of Jesus Christ. His essential ordinances bind us to Him through sacred priesthood covenants. Then, as we keep our covenants, He endows us with His healing, strengthening power."[3]

After the Seoul Korea Temple was dedicated, my mom worked as an ordinance worker every Friday after work, and my grandma attended the temple every Thursday. My grandma continued attending as often as her body allowed her until she passed away at age 100.

Obtaining Genealogy Books

We continue doing genealogy work because we love doing it. There is so much to do, and we do not have enough time. After some opposition, my family has obtained twenty-some books of my mom's side of genealogy records. We have been working on this set of twenty-some books for decades, with further thirty-volume records for the Kwon side. I have those to work on for the rest of my life.

Entering Names of Ancestors

Since receiving her patriarchal blessing, sharing the gospel with family and relatives has always been on my mom's mind. My mom reads the records that are written in Chinese characters and writes them on a separate piece of paper. By 2007, my mom had hundreds of sheets written, which meant tens of thousands of names waiting to be entered. Back then, GEDCOM files were made first. Then, those files were sent to a Korean sister, Sister Seong, who worked in the Family History Center, to upload to the Church genealogy system. I started feeling I needed to do genealogy and enter those names into the GEDCOM system. My sister even bought me a computer to do that, but I didn't jump right into it.

Apparently, my ancestors were getting impatient. In the summer of 2007, I was laid off from my job. I was angry for less than a second. Then a clear and strong impression came, "*Perfect! I can do genealogy!*" I could never quit a job without lining up a new job because my mom would bury me alive. However, by divine intervention, I got six months of uninterrupted time to do genealogy. I knew this time was given to me to enter those names of my ancestors. The first couple of days, I was getting the feel of how long it would take to enter those names. I calculated if I entered about 1,000 names a day, I could finish it in six months. I prayed and asked Heavenly Father that I would not get a job before I finished entering the names. I did this every day. I woke up and entered the names. It was like a full-time job. Those six months were the most spiritual and happiest time in my life, even more spiritual than being a missionary or an MTC teacher. It took a little under six months to finish. A week after I finished, I got a job offer. In the Lord's mysterious way, He turned an unpleasant situation into a life-changing experience.

Doing this genealogy has made me feel closer to my ancestors. In 2010, I got into a car accident, which could have been a serious one, but no one was badly injured. After the accident, my cousin, Euseung, Aunt Kee Hong's son, who was living in Provo, came and gave me a blessing. In that blessing, I was told that my ancestors were watching over me. My heart fills with love for my ancestors as I continue doing genealogy work.

My family decided to share all the names we've submitted with the temple and prayed the ordinances would be done someday. Nothing happened to those names for a long time. Then I started seeing some of the ordinances being done, like two to three ordinances a day. Then, it picked up the pace. As of February 2024, about 17,000 ancestors' ordinances had been completed in less than a year.

It is amazing, humbling, and terrifying at the same time to see how fast ordinances are done in temples all around the world. There is power in teamwork. The power of God that moves things and people for His work to be done is beyond imagination and is awe-striking. I am utterly nothing, less than dirt, in the presence of His power. What my family and I do to gather and submit names is the least we can do.

Love

The love of God and our love for Him turn us to our ancestors. Elder Groberg also said in his talk, "Responding to true love is part of our very being. We innately desire to reconnect here with the love we felt there. Only as we feel God's love and fill our hearts with His love can we be truly happy . . . God is anxious to help us feel His love wherever we are."[4]

For example, after finishing my second emphasis in graphic design, I had difficulty finding a desirable job. I applied to so many places, but I didn't get the job I wanted. I was so angry. I was in the depths of despair. I knew I shouldn't be because I would be turning my back on God. Those words came to my mind at that time. But I was still angry at God for not giving me the job I wanted. I was fuming and crying in the bathroom.

Then, in my head, not physically, but like a vision, I saw a bright light on the right side of my head and heard a clear yet gentle voice saying, "*I love you.*" Those simple words caught me off guard. What did that have to do with me in my situation? Then I heard it again, but this time I heard, "*I love you. I want you to be happy.*" I knew, then, precisely what that meant—everything made sense. All the so-called failures and rejections were not God tormenting me, but it was me tormenting myself and misunderstanding Him, who is a loving Father in Heaven. He only wants me to be happy. Instead of giving me a fancy job somewhere, He gave me an understanding of His love and divine identity as a daughter of God. It was another time of perspective shift.

Elder Groberg continued, "When we understand who God is, who we are, how He loves us, and what His plan is for us, fear evaporates. When we get the tiniest glimpse of these truths, our concern over worldly things vanishes. . . . We cannot fake love. It must become part of us. . . . Jesus Christ was filled with unfathomable love as He endured incomprehensible pain, cruelty, and injustice for us. Through His love for us, He rose above otherwise insurmountable barriers. His love knows no barriers. He invites us to follow Him and partake of His unlimited love so we too may rise above the pain and cruelty and injustice of this world and help and forgive and bless."[5]

NOTES

Adapted from a devotional address given at BYU–Hawaii.

1. John H. Groberg, "The Power of God's Love," *Ensign* or *Liahona*, November 2004.
2. Benjamín de Hoyos, "The Work of the Temple and Family History—One and the Same Work," *Liahona*, May 2023.
3. Russell M. Nelson, "The Temple and Your Spiritual Foundation," *Liahona*, November 2021.
4. Groberg, "The Power of God's Love."
5. Groberg, "The Power of God's Love."

YOU WERE MADE TO SPEAK UP

And Esther answered, If it seem good unto the king, let the king and Haman come this day unto the banquet that I have prepared for him.

Then the king said, Cause Haman to make haste, that he may do as Esther hath said. So the king and Haman came to the banquet that Esther had prepared.

And the king said unto Esther at the banquet of wine, What is thy petition? and it shall be granted thee: and what is thy request? even to the half of the kingdom it shall be performed.

Then answered Esther, and said, My petition and my request is; If I have found favour in the sight of the king, and if it please the king to grant my petition, and to perform my request, let the king and Haman come to the banquet that I shall prepare for them, and I will do to morrow as the king hath said. (Esther 5:4-8)

THE MIDDLE OF THE STORY

Sarah Sun

SARAH SUN was Miss Utah 2023 and the Student Body President of BYU from 2024 to 2025. She served in the Mormon Battalion Historic Site and California Riverside Missions. She grew up in Southern Utah, where she met her sweetheart, Ted Kanell. They were sealed in the Bountiful Utah Temple in 2024.

All great stories have conflict. Can you imagine if Cinderella's father never died?

"Once upon a time there was a nice girl who came from a loving family, lived a good life, married a rich guy, and always maxed out her 401k. The end."

Or imagine if Barbie never had to venture into the real world? "Once upon a time, Margot Robbie was gorgeous. The end."

And what if Jean Valjean had not been faced with the dilemma of stealing a loaf of bread to feed his starving family? Everyone still would have been miserable, but it certainly would have been a much shorter novel.

We all understand that conflict is what makes a story great. The stories that we like are the ones that highlight humankind's remarkable capacity to overcome adversity. Those are the stories that elevate our souls, inspire us to greater heights, and provide trenchant insight into the human experience.

Stories like that usually have a similar structure. When we find our protagonist faced with a seemingly impossible challenge, we become even more invested in their success, even more excited to see how things play out, and even more eager to relish in their vindication because we expect things to work out. They have to! From the first two snare drums of the 20th Century Fox intro, we already know that things will probably turn out fine. Instead of dread or despondency, we feel exhilaration as our hero or heroine fights their battles. We believe in them. And we know how things are going to end.

Sisters, we know how things are going to end. Yet, when we find ourselves in the middle of our own stories, when tension is mounting and hope is waning, we may be tempted to question whether Heavenly Father is still the "author and finisher of our story."[1] Without seeing the finished product of our lives, we may question whether we are still in the Savior's hands. The middle of the story is a tricky place to be. But when we find our commitment and devotion to our heavenly parents faltering during our trials, walking with the Savior allows us to recenter, refocus, and renew our faith in the Master Plan.

My message today is for anyone who feels like they might be in the middle of their story. As Latter-day Saints, we know the fulness of our Father's glorious plan for His children. Before we came to this earth, we dwelt with our Father in Heaven. Having made promises with God before the earth was even formed, we had faith in his plan. We knew full well who and what we were going to become: gods and goddesses, like our heavenly parents.

As we walk with the Spirit, we can feel gentle assurance that we are on the right path. We are endowed with enabling power from on high as we make and keep sacred covenants. Yet despite the plethora of evidence that substantiates God's love, there will still be times when we doubt. There will still be times when we are tempted to curse Him during His perceived absence. If you find yourself wondering if you've messed everything up, remember that you are not that powerful. Remember that your story is not over yet. If you get anything from this talk, let it be this: do not falter before you reach the finish line. When your faith begins to waver, cling even tighter to the promises He has made unto you. We did not elect to come to earth because we thought it would be easy. We came to earth having already chosen the harder path, knowing that only by experiencing what they did can we become as they are.

We cannot become like our heavenly parents without experiencing what has made them divine. Mortality, and the pain that often accompanies it, was designed with a purpose in mind. Think about how often people curse the name of God. How often our heavenly parents are mischaracterized by those they love. Think about the heartbreak loving parents feel as they witness their perfect Son be rejected, bullied, and betrayed. The loneliness that comes from being misunderstood at the hands of willful ignorance. Think of our Savior reaching out for succor in the Garden of Gethsemane, knowing that the only way out was through, and the only way through was complete reliance on the Father. When we find ourselves in the thick of our trials, we must not lose hope. It's the middle of the story when the plot begins to get good.

With all this talk of stories, I figured I would tell you a little bit of mine.

I grew up an Evangelical Baptist in a small town in southern Utah, with no intention of ever joining the Church. To put things into perspective, my youth group once hosted a white elephant gift party. The pastor didn't want to place a financial burden on anyone, so he said, "Don't worry about bringing a fancy gift. Bring something cheap! You know, just bring something that no one else would even want!"

I really took that to heart. "Hmm, what's something that no one else wants?"

And showed up with a Book of Mormon.

Having attended dozens of presentations about why the Church was false, the takeaway that always stuck with me was simply to avoid the missionaries at all costs. I can't tell you the number of times when the elders would knock on my door, we would make eye contact through the window, and then I'd duck underneath the piano bench with the audacity to pretend like we did not just acknowledge each other's existence.

With volumes of anti-Latter-day Saint literature under my belt and having fielded dozens of invitations by neighbors to attend Church and Church activities, I thought I knew it all. That is, until a fateful interaction in the holy land of Provo, Utah, at the age of fourteen.

I was sitting at the front of a school bus on my way back to

Cedar City when I felt a tug telling me to talk to the girl in the seat next to me.

I couldn't think of anything to say, so I asked her about the gold medallion hanging around her neck. I'll let you all in on a little secret. I knew all about the Personal Progress medallion and had been invited to participate in the program prior to the interaction. But I put on my best act of feigned ignorance and asked her to tell me about the temple on her necklace.

You see, the words she said were words I had heard before. But hearing her bear her testimony of the restored gospel made me feel something completely different. The way she lived her life and her sincere belief in the gospel of Jesus Christ allowed her to be a powerful vessel for the Spirit to break through the calcified shell around my heart. Listening to her speak, I could not deny that I felt something I had never felt before. While I couldn't identify the feeling at the time, I now know that it was the Holy Ghost prompting me to continue asking questions, to continue seeking after truth, to continue questioning my assumptions about the nature of God, myself, and life.

Eventually my questions led to a different friend inviting me to meet with the missionaries. She simply asked, "Sarah, will you meet with the missionaries?" I replied, "Absolutely not." To which she responded, "Awesome. They will be at your house on Tuesday at seven!"

Three years and hundreds of questions later, I made the pivotal decision to embark on the covenant path and was baptized at the age of seventeen. I knew that joining the Church would not make things easier for me. It would entail losing friends, a community, and a lifestyle. Yet, as a new convert, there was nothing more important to me than living and sharing the gospel. I knew the Church was true, and I was ready to walk on burning coals for Jesus. Following my freshman year of college at my dream school, I decided to serve a mission, where I received an undeniable prompting to transfer to BYU. At that point I had learned better than to deny a prompting, so I obeyed, not knowing why or how or whether things would work out. That brings me here, to the present moment, where I am now in the middle of my own story.

Without knowing what the future holds, I have been reflecting a lot on the past. On this topic, President Jeffrey R. Holland states:

> The past is to be learned from but not lived in. We look back to claim the embers from glowing experiences but not the ashes. And when we have learned what we need to learn and have brought with us the best that we have experienced, then we look ahead, we remember that *faith is always pointed toward the future.* Faith always has to do with blessings and truths and events that will *yet* be efficacious in our lives.[2]

On the pathway of discipleship, all of us will make difficult decisions. Do not allow the faith-filled choices you've made pale in the face of fear. Faith is heroic, despite the world bombarding you with messages that state otherwise. The world will tell you that not abiding by its value system is foolish. But Abraham, Sarah, Lehi, and Sariah all left behind tremendous wealth, status, and notoriety to be pioneers in the kingdom of God. Imagine how worn out they must have been by ridicule from their communities and resentment by their own family members, especially considering that they did not live long enough to witness the payoff. Yet, they pressed forward.

As children of the covenant tasked with gathering Israel in this last dispensation, we all have the potential to be pioneers of faith, courageous and bold in our conviction. Being a disciple of Christ is not for the faint of heart, and choosing the right will inevitably lead to leaving something of lesser value behind. From President Holland again:

> It is possible that Lot's wife looked back with resentment toward the Lord for what He was asking her to leave behind. . . . It isn't just that she looked back; she looked back *longingly.* In short, her attachment to the past outweighed her confidence in the future. . . . Some of you were having thoughts such as these: Is there any future for me? What does a new year or a new semester or a new major or a new romance hold for me? Will I be safe? Will life be sound? Can I trust in the Lord and in the future? Or would it be better to look back, to go back, to go home? To all such of every generation, I call out, "Remember Lot's wife." Faith is for the future. Faith builds on the past but never longs to stay there. Faith trusts that God has great things in store for each of us and that Christ truly is the "high priest of good things to come" (Hebrews 9:11).[3]

Today is the day to strengthen your resolve. Today is the day to look forward with faith. And to anyone struggling to press forward, remember that the middle of the story oftentimes feels like the end.

Because in the middle of the story, Eve ruined everything.

In the middle of the story, Joseph was rotting in prison.

In the middle of the story, Noah built a boat for a storm that wasn't coming.

Moses wandered for forty years.

Hannah was infertile.

Isaac was not coming back from that hike.

Jonah got stuck in a whale.

Mary was going to get broken up with.

Bethesda was too far.

The Egyptians were too close.

It was just mud.

Lazarus was dead.

And Jesus Christ underwhelmed the Jewish nation, was hung on a cross, and dashed all hopes of the revolution that had been hoped for for thousands of years.

Everybody was ready to close the book on these stories—the end, game over. But if there's one thing we learn from the scriptures, it's that we can never place a period where God has placed a comma. When all other options have been worn out, when circumstances can't get worse, when everything else has failed, get ready, because that is *exactly* when God shows up.

Because Joseph became second-in-command.

The entire earth flooded.

Milk and honey were everywhere.

Hannah rejoiced.

Isaac was spared.

Ninevah repented.

Mary became the mother of the Messiah.

The paralytic leapt.

The Red Sea parted.

The blind man washed his face and could see.

Lazarus was just kidding.

And Jesus Christ pulled off the resurrection, defeating sin and death. And the earth that Eve thought she ruined was restored for all eternity.

With God, your mess will become a message. With God, your test will become a testimony, your trial will become a triumph, and your victimhood will become a victory.

Refuse to turn the page when God's pen is still on the paper. When you find yourself in the middle of your story, when tension is mounting and hope is waning, remember:

We know how this ends.

NOTES

Adapted from a talk given at BYU Women's Conference.

1. Camille N. Johnson, "Invite Christ to Author Your Story," *Liahona*, November 2021.
2. Jeffrey R. Holland, "Remember Lot's Wife," Brigham Young University devotional, January 13, 2009, speeches.byu.edu.
3. Holland, "Remember Lot's Wife."

YOU WERE MADE TO BE BOLD

So the king and Haman came to banquet with Esther the queen. And the king said again unto Esther . . . What is thy petition, queen Esther? and it shall be granted thee: and what is thy request? and it shall be performed, even to the half of the kingdom.

Then Esther the queen answered and said, If I have found favour in thy sight, O king, and if it please the king, let my life be given me at my petition, and my people at my request: For we are sold, I and my people, to be destroyed, to be slain, and to perish. But if we had been sold for bondmen and bondwomen, I had held my tongue, although the enemy could not countervail the king's damage.

Then the king Ahasuerus answered and said unto Esther the queen, Who is he, and where is he, that durst presume in his heart to do so?

And Esther said, The adversary and enemy is this wicked Haman. (Esther 7:1-6)

I WILL TRUST IN THEE FOREVER

Jennifer Kerns Davis

JENNIFER KERNS DAVIS grew up in the mountains of Arizona, Idaho, New Mexico, and Utah. She is wife to Jesse, mother to three children, and grandmother to one grandchild. Jennifer can identify most mountain wildflowers by name, and she often prays for a growing collection of friends who also have children living on the other side of the veil.

There is a verse in 2 Nephi 4 that becomes an anthem to women, men, youth, and children in every corner of the earth and throughout all time of faith, trust, and commitment to our Lord. It says, "Lord, I have trusted in thee, and I will trust in thee forever" (2 Nephi 4:34). It is an affirmation offered to us through scripture that we can repeat as we meditate or when we need to give ourselves a pep talk as we endure with trust each day or each minute.

Nephi needed this affirmation. His father, perhaps the person who understood him best, had just passed away, and Nephi was grieving. People in his family were in the process of leaving the Church, and it's likely he felt the looming detachment of some of his dear brothers, sisters, and nieces and nephews as the family separated. I envision Nephi feeling pain as his children grieved their grandfather.

In his discouragement, he got down on himself, calling himself "wretched" (2 Nephi 4:17). We might even hear hints of depression in verse 26: "My heart weep[s] and my soul linger[s] in the valley of sorrow . . . my strength slacken[s], because of my afflictions." In these verses, Nephi is feeling very, very low.

Have you ever felt this way? I have—several times. I felt low after a divorce, and from time to time as I was a single mother for eleven years, again when I was diagnosed with a serious illness, as I've worried for my children, struggled at work, and generally here and there throughout my life. But these last twenty months have been the hardest.

Twenty months ago, our family experienced something that changed our lives forever. Our oldest child, Parker, passed to the next life by suicide. The grief I've felt has affected my physical health, my confidence, my relationships—and it's been painful to see my family members and Parker's friends around me grieve.

I've learned that it's easy to lose yourself in the grief, and it's been hard for me to figure out myself again. I've realized how easy it is for Satan to encompass you about as he did Nephi, (see 2 Nephi 18:4). And I've learned that trusting in the Lord is sometimes all you have.

In fact, looking back through every one of my trials, I've realized that trusting in the Lord has allowed Him to lift me and make me even stronger than I ever was before. 2 Nephi 4, which is sometimes called "the psalm of Nephi," has been a comfort to me throughout my life. Even Nephi's apparent feelings of depression have been comforting—to show that I'm not the only one that has ever felt that way. And it's motivating that the words he uses in positive self-talk to pick himself up can also be used by anyone else.

"Awake, my soul!" he says, in verse 28. "Rejoice, O my heart!" Then he recounts the numberless ways God has blessed him and delivered on His promises. Nephi remembers that God trusts him in verses 17 and 23. In verse 21, he remembers he is loved with the most perfect love that could ever exist—God's love! He remembers that he has been prepared for this moment of trial in verses 24 and 25, and then he prays to God and asks for more strength, courage, capability, and power from the Lord to overcome the world. He ends his psalm with more trust-phrases: "I know that God will give liberally to him that asketh. . . . My voice shall forever ascend up unto thee." Then, empowered, Nephi continues forward in his life with a piece of God's strength in him.

This chapter becomes a pattern for us to use when we also need empowerment. Nephi's psalm is a clear model to make important things happen with our faith.

First, let's look at how Nephi used affirmations and declarations for positive-self talk. Now, I know that affirmations alone don't get you out of a depression, but they do help you move in a better direction. I need positive affirmations all the time to motivate myself to do what I came here to Earth to do!

Listen to some of these trust affirmations found throughout the scriptures:

"God is my salvation; I will trust, and not be afraid" (Isaiah 12:2).

"In God I have put my trust; I will not be afraid what man can do unto me" (Psalm 56:11).

"The God of my rock; in him will I trust: he is my shield, and the horn of my salvation, my high tower, and my refuge, my saviour" (2 Samuel 22:3).

Let's look at Matthew 15:28, when the woman of Canaan comes to Jesus and asks that her daughter be healed. Jesus says something He might say to each one of us, in an affirmation or declaration straight from Him: "O woman, great is thy faith: be it unto thee even as thou wilt." Imagine Christ saying that to you.

Here is another affirmation: "The Lord in his great and infinite goodness doth bless and prosper those who put their trust in him" (Helaman 12:1). We might say, He will bless and prosper me when I put my trust in Him.

We can follow Nephi's example of trust by remembering our past blessings and when God has delivered us.

Elder Anderson calls these remembrances "spiritually defining memories," and he says this about them: "God powerfully and very personally assures each of us that He knows us and loves us and that He is blessing us specifically and openly. Then, in our moments of difficulty, the Savior brings these experiences back into our mind."[1]

Remembering when we've trusted God in the past can help remind us that God can be trusted in the present and the future. We can create our own records of trust. Nephi, Elder Anderson, and President Eyring all testify that writing down their "spiritually defining memories" helped to increase their trust in the Lord.[2] I would also like to testify of this. I tenderly share with you that I'm keeping a record of God's promises to me. But first I need to tell you about a particular recent promise God made to me.

The day Parker passed away, when I first found out Parker was in trouble, and after calling dispatch for help, I hit my knees and pleaded with God from the painful depths of my soul, "God! Father! I need a miracle!" I repeated my plea with fervency until I gradually calmed and humbly asked God if he would please grant me the miracle I was seeking.

And then, I knew. I knew I needed to ask for a "but if not," because I knew that miracle wasn't going to happen (see Daniel 3:17–18). I understood that God respected Parker's agency, but I didn't know what "but if not" to ask for. And so I asked God if He could give me the "but if not." The answer I received was this: "There are more miracles, bigger miracles, and better miracles than the one you are asking for." He was asking me to trust Him, even though what I wanted more than anything in that moment was to have my boy. But because He'd already demonstrated He was trustworthy through other life experiences and in the scriptures, I knew that the all-powerful God of the universe could do what He promised! So I mustered up my mustard seed of trust, and called up every ounce of courage in my broken heart, thinking of the more, bigger, and better miracles He was promising me. God has not backed down from that promise! I want to never, ever forget God's promises, because there's another promise God has made to me: that I will see my little boy again! I'm doing my best to keep a record of His trustworthiness, His kindness, His mercy, and His love.

Another way to remember how the Lord has blessed you is to look back on when He has prepared you for what you're currently doing. My favorite part of the account of David and Goliath is that God gave David opportunities to practice before his encounter with Goliath. God sent David a bear and a lion to fight so he knew God would help him fight Goliath (see 1 Samuel 17:34–37). Similarly, God gives us preparations because He wants us to feel confident as we tackle the trials before us. You can trust God to prepare you, and looking back on how He has prepared you for a particular moment can give you courage to move forward.

Reading or recalling the trust-testimonies found in the scriptures can also provide encouragement to us:

- God promised the Israelites that He would deliver them from Egyptian captivity. And then He did! (see Exodus 6:6–8 and the books of Exodus, Leviticus, and Deuteronomy).
- He promised Nephi's mother, father, sisters, and brothers multiple times that He would take them to a promised land to escape the fall of Jerusalem, and then He did! (see 1 Nephi 2:2 and 1 Nephi 18:23).
- God promised he would restore the gospel of Jesus Christ to its fullness after apostasy, and then He did! (see 1 Nephi 13:26–29 and Joseph Smith—History 1:1–20).
- God promised us that He would send us a Savior to show us a better way to live and to redeem us from sin and death and then He did! (see Moses 4:1 and John 17:4).

"God is powerful to the fulfilling of all his words. For he will fulfill all his promises which he shall make unto you, for he has fulfilled his promises which he has made unto our fathers" (Alma 37:16–17).

The scriptures are records of how God keeps His promises. The scriptures are books of trust. In fact, Moroni both starts and ends the Book of Mormon indicating that the entire book is an account of God's Hand in the lives of His children. The title page of the Book of Mormon says the book's purpose is "to show unto the remnant of the house of Israel what great things the Lord hath done for their fathers," while the last chapter in the Book of Mormon implores us to "remember how merciful the Lord hath been unto the children of men, from the creation of Adam even down until the time that ye shall receive these things, and ponder it in your hearts" (Moroni 10:3).

When we look at trust examples from prophets or the people around us, we have to beware the temptation to think something like, "Yeah, but that was Moses. I'm no Moses, I'm just Jen." Do not diminish your faith. We can't let ourselves listen to the lie that hope and trust and faith don't apply to us because we are "normal" or "regular." Listen to Jesus Christ's counsel to us: "If ye have faith as a grain of mustard seed, ye shall say unto this mountain, Remove hence to yonder place; and it shall remove; and nothing shall be impossible unto you" (Matthew 17:20). Note that He doesn't say "nothing shall be impossible unto the prophets." He says *you*!

With that in mind, our faith must be in the Savior and not in a desired outcome. The scriptures teach us not to counsel the Lord, and that His blessings will come to us "in his own time, and in his own way, and according to his own will" (Doctrine and Covenants 88:68). I take that to mean that we should not tell Him how or when to do His job, or to expect that He will deliver us in the same way He's delivered others. God's delivery looks different for everyone.

For years, my husband and I have prayed that our children would be blessed with experiences that would lead them to the Savior. Since Parker has moved to the other side of the veil, we have received very sacred and real manifestations that Parker's experiences on this side and the other side of the veil have led him to the Savior. I recognize God is blessing our family in a very special way, particular to our circumstance, and I have no doubt he will compensate us for every loss because He said he would. In His omniscient love, He delivers differently, but assuredly, He delivers. I know He will do the same for you.

President Nelson shared: "Please know this: if everything and everyone else in the world whom you trust should fail, Jesus Christ and His Church will never fail you. He will not forsake His covenants, His promises, or His love for His people. He works miracles today, and He will work miracles tomorrow."[3]

Now, with all this talk of trusting in the Lord, we should talk about how He reciprocates it with us. He trusts us! One example of a scripture proving this can be found in Doctrine and Covenants 9:8: "But, behold, I say unto you, that you must study it out in your mind; then you must ask me if it be right, and if it is right I will cause that your bosom shall burn within you; therefore, you shall feel that it is right." I love to paraphrase this scripture this way as counsel from God: "You are smart, intuitive, and have inherited my spiritual DNA. I trust you. And I want to cocreate your life with you."

He trusts us to make decisions and to influence each other. He trusts us to love, to learn, and to grow. He even trusts us to "conquer Satan" in our lives by seeking His divine help (see Doctrine and Covenants 10:5). He trusts in our ability to rely on Him to change and to overcome the world and to humble ourselves. He really does trust us!

Whether you realize it or not, you are already trusting in the Lord. If you've made covenants with God, you are trusting in the Lord. If you've ever served a mission, or sent a child or parents or a friend on a mission, you are trusting in the Lord. If you've ever accepted a calling, acted on a prompting, prayed, searched for answers, you are trusting in the Lord. If you've ever hauled your family to church late with someone in your family's hair sticking up and their shirt untucked, you are trusting in the Lord. Don't minimize the trust you already have in the Lord! Don't let the adversary take that from you. You are trusting in the Lord!

Now, that being said, if you ever feel like you'd like a little more trust, or if you ever feel that your trust at times is wavering, pray and ask for the spiritual gift of trusting in the Lord. We are encouraged by the Lord in the Doctrine and Covenants to seek earnestly the best spiritual gifts to improve our lives and the lives of those whom we serve (see Doctrine and Covenants 46:8). The ability to trust in the Lord is one of these spiritual gifts.

We've been counseled to use our spiritual gifts to bless the lives of others. Can I introduce you to two of the cutest little old ladies I've ever known? The use of their spiritual gifts to trust in the Lord impacted my life and the lives of my family in a chain of trust that knows no end.

Mary King Timothy and Leone Nance Gardner lived in Kaysville, Utah, as across-the-street neighbors. This narrative of trust began when they put their time and lives in the Lord's hands by requesting mission calls while in their seventies. Having both been called to the Arizona Phoenix mission, these two missionaries were serving together in Sedona, Arizona, when they knocked on the door of Earl and Jeri Kerns.

My mother, a member of the Church, married my dad five years earlier, and had prayed for those five years that one day my father would become converted to the gospel of Jesus Christ.

She wanted to be together forever with her family. The Lord told her to trust. On the day and the very minute Sisters Timothy and Gardner came to our home to introduce themselves, my mother was fulfilling her responsibilities as a ministering sister.

My father unsuspectingly opened the door at home to those dear missionaries, asking if they could come in. My dad's heart melted because just two years before, his beloved Granny Hooper had passed through the veil, and, while he had declined invitations previously to meet with several sets of elders, his resistance was no match for two little grandmas who reminded him of his granny.

When my mother came home from ministering, she met these missionaries and was shocked to find out that they had already made an appointment for a return visit! My father realized he would need to pray to ask God if he should join The Church of Jesus Christ of Latter-day Saints. So, one October Sunday in 1978, my dad walked to a small grove of Gambel oak trees and prayed, believing he would get an answer.

At the end of the day, my dad came into the house, and without saying a word to his family, picked up the phone and dialed a number. My mom waited in suspense until the missionaries answered on the other line and my dad exclaimed: "What's a guy gotta do in this town to get baptized?"

A few weeks later, he did get baptized. It was a defining childhood memory for me, as was our sealing a year later.

There's one last aspect of trust to this story I'd like to share. While these missionaries were exercising their trust to serve the Lord, remember—they left daughters, sons, and grandchildren at home. Each one of them, exercising their trust in the Lord, released their mother or grandmother in the Lord's service to make this miracle of faith happen for a family they'd never met.

Do you see the chain of trust that occurred here? The trust of the missionaries, their families, my mother, my father, and my father's granny all came together to help our family commence on the covenant path. Can you imagine the chain of trust that could form for our own families, in our wards and stakes, among our neighborhoods, and across our world as we unite our faith and trust in the Lord? We can and must make important things happen by our faith!

A painting by Katie Garner called *My Yoke Is Easy, My Burden Is Light* is one of my all-time favorite paintings of the Savior. It shows Jesus looking at us and smiling while lifting half of a wooden yoke. He is yoked with me, with you, with anyone who wishes to have the Savior's strength and power as they pull their load. He is joyful that we have asked to be yoked with Him! Starting at baptism and continuing with the covenants in temple, we can invite the Savior to share our yoke. As we continue keeping and honoring those covenants, He can continue to share our burden.

Here's what President Russell M. Nelson has said about this: "Entering into a covenant relationship with God binds us to Him in a way that makes everything about life easier. Please do not misunderstand me: I did not say that making covenants makes life easy. But yoking yourself with the Savior means you have access to His strength and redeeming power."[4]

And President Emily Belle Freeman's counsel only seconds this: "We must remember: it's not the course alone that will exalt us; it's the companion—our Savior. And *this* is the why of the covenant relationship."[5]

So after we make covenants that secure us to the Savior, how do we strengthen the relationships we have with our Heavenly Father and Jesus Christ? We just spend time with them. I invite you to ask God what way of spending time with Him would best deepen your relationship with Him.

The words of our church leaders lately are peppered with beautiful invitations to deepen our relationship with our Lord Jesus Christ and God, our Father. Here are just a few:

From President Nelson: "The more you learn about the Savior, the easier it will be to trust in His mercy, His infinite love, and His strengthening, healing, and redeeming power."[6] "Put yourself in a position to begin having experiences with Him. Humble yourself. Pray to have eyes to see God's hand in your life and in the world around you. Ask Him to tell you if He is really there—if He knows you. Ask Him how He feels about you. And then listen."[7]

From Sister J. Annette Dennis: "Covenants create the kind of relationship that allows God to mold and change us over time and lift us to become more like the Savior."⁸

Elder Kearon testified: "God is in relentless pursuit of you."⁹

And Christ himself said, "Come unto me" (Matthew 11:28).

Our Savior Jesus Christ wants us close to Him—as close as we can get. Our Redeemer and our Heavenly Father love us, and They want us to spend time with Them, so They can spend time with us. We can grow to know Them. They are infinitely good, and kind, and merciful. They are caring, loving and full of grace. They are strong and powerful and protective.

A study of the scriptures with the express purpose of coming to know God the Father and His Son Jesus Christ will change everything. Mark every word that notes their names, their attributes, their actions, and their words, and you will come to know of the intense loving care they have for you.¹⁰

We *are* the women who know how to make important things happen by our faith. And you know how we can do it? We're going to remember our past blessings. We're going to ask for the spiritual gift of trust. We're going to put our faith in the Lord, and not in an outcome. We are going to make and keep covenants that secure us with the Savior and His Atonement. We are going to intentionally look for ways to build relationships with our Heavenly Father and Jesus Christ. And we are going to look over in our yoke at our Savior as He cheers us on and eases our load.

NOTES

Adapted from a talk given at BYU Women's Conference.

1. Neil L. Anderson, "Spiritually Defining Memories," *Liahona*, May 2020.

2. See Henry B. Eyring, "O Remember, Remember," *Ensign* or *Liahona*, November 2007.
3. Russell M. Nelson, "Christ is Risen; Faith in Him Will Move Mountains," *Liahona*, May 2021.
4. Russell M. Nelson, "Overcome the World and Find Rest," *Liahona*, November 2022.
5. Emily Belle Freeman, "Walking in Covenant Relationship with Christ," *Liahona*, November 2023.
6. Russell M. Nelson, "Christ is Risen; Faith in Him Will Move Mountains," *Liahona*, November 2021.
7. Russell M. Nelson, "Come, Follow Me," *Ensign* or *Liahona*, November 2019.
8. J. Annette Dennis, "Put Ye On the Lord Jesus Christ," *Liahona*, May 2024.
9. Patrick Kearon, "God's Intent Is to Bring You Home," *Liahona*, May 2024.
10. You might consider getting an inexpensive paperback copy of the scriptures and using four different colors to mark these four things: 1) Their names, 2) Their attributes, 3) Their actions, 4) Their words. Note also the number of pages that have at least one of these items marked. The scriptures truly are a record of God's hand in our lives.

YOU WERE MADE TO STAND FOR WHAT'S RIGHT

And [Esther] said, If it please the king, and if I have found favour in his sight, and the thing seem right before the king, and I be pleasing in his eyes, let it be written to reverse the letters devised by Haman the son of Hammedatha the Agagite, which he wrote to destroy the Jews which are in all the king's provinces: For how can I endure to see the evil that shall come unto my people? or how can I endure to see the destruction of my kindred? (Esther 8:5-6)

BECOMING WOMEN OF GREATER FAITH IN CHRIST

Patricia T. Holland

PATRICIA HOLLAND (1942–2023) was a Latter-day Saint writer and leader. She was a member of the General Presidency of the Young Women organization and also "first lady" of Brigham Young University, where her husband, Jeffery R. Holland, was president. The Hollands are the parents of three children.

Just after my release from the Young Women general presidency in April 1986, I had the opportunity to spend a week in Israel. It had been a very difficult and demanding two years for me. In an important period of forming principles and starting programs, I worried that I wasn't doing enough—and I tried to run a little faster.

Toward the end of my two-year term, my health was going downhill. I was losing weight steadily, and I wasn't sleeping well. And yet, I kept wondering what I might have done to manage it all better. The brethren extended a loving release. As grateful as my family was for the conclusion of my term of service, I nevertheless felt a loss of association—and, I confess, some loss of identity—with those women that I had come to love so much. Who was I, and where was I in this welter of demands? Should life be as hard as all this? The days after my release were about as difficult as the weeks before it. I didn't have any reserve to call on. My tank was on empty, and I wasn't sure there was a filling station anywhere in sight.

It was just a few weeks later that my husband had the assignment in Jerusalem to which I have referred, and the brethren traveling on the assignment requested that I accompany him. "Come on," he said. "You can recuperate in the Savior's land of living water and bread of life." As weary as I was, I packed my bags, believing—or, at the very least, hoping—that the time there would be a healing respite.

On a pristinely clear and beautifully bright day, I sat overlooking the Sea of Galilee and reread the tenth chapter of Luke. But instead of the words on the page, I thought I saw with my mind and heard with my heart these words: "[Pat, Pat, Pat], thou art careful and troubled about many things." Then the power of pure and personal revelation seized me as I read, "But one thing [only one thing] is [truly] needful" (Luke 10:42).

The May sun in Israel is so bright you feel as if you are sitting on top of the world. I had just visited the spot in Bethoron where the sun stood still for Joshua (see Joshua 10:12), and indeed, on that day, it seemed so for me as well. As I sat pondering my problems I felt that same sun's healing rays like warm liquid pouring into my heart—relaxing, calming, and comforting my troubled soul.

Our loving Father in Heaven seemed to be whispering to me,

"You don't have to worry over so many things. The one thing that is needful—the *only* thing that is truly needful—is to keep your eyes toward the sun—my Son." Suddenly I had true peace. I knew that my life had always been in His hands—from the very beginning! The sea lying peacefully before my eyes had been tempest-tossed and dangerous—many, many times. All I needed to do was to renew my faith and get a firm grasp on his hand—and *together* we could walk on the water.

I would like to pose a question for each of us to ponder. How do we as women make that leap from being troubled and worried to being women of even greater faith? One frame of mind surely seems to negate the other. Faith and fear cannot long coexist. Consider some of the things that trouble us.

I have served as a Relief Society president in four different wards. Two of these wards were for single women, and two were wards with many young mothers. As I sat in counsel with my single sisters, my heart often ached as they described to me their feelings of loneliness and disappointment. They felt that their lives had no meaning or purpose in a church that rightly puts so much emphasis on marriage and family life. Most painful of all was the occasional suggestion that their singleness was their own fault—or worse yet, a selfish desire. They were anxiously seeking for peace and purpose—something of real value to which they could dedicate their lives.

Yet it seemed to me that the young mothers had easily as many concerns. They described to me the struggles of trying to raise children in an increasingly difficult world, of never having enough time or means or freedom to feel like a person of value. And there were so few tangible evidences that what they were doing was really going to be successful. There was no one to give them a raise in pay; and beyond their husbands, no one to compliment them on a job well done. And they were always tired! The one thing I remember so vividly with these young mothers was that they were *always* so tired.

Then there were those women who, through no fault of their own, found themselves the sole provider for their homes financially, spiritually, emotionally, and in every other way. I could not even comprehend the challenges they faced. Obviously, in some ways, theirs was the most demanding circumstance of all. The perspective I have gained over these many years of listening to the worries of women is that no one woman or group of women—single, married, divorced, widowed, homemakers, or professionals—have cornered the market on concerns. There seem to be plenty of challenges to go around. But, I hasten to add, there are marvelous blessings as well.

Every one of us has privileges and blessings, and every one of us has fears and trials. It seems bold to say, but common sense suggests that never before in the history of the world have women, including LDS women, been faced with greater complexity in their concerns.

Obviously the Lord has created us with different personalities, as well as differing degrees of energy, interest, health, talent, and opportunity. So long as we are committed to righteousness and living a life of faithful devotion, we should celebrate these divine differences, knowing they are a gift from God. We must not feel so frightened, so threatened and insecure; we must not need to find exact replicas of ourselves in order to feel validated as women of worth. There are many things over which we can be divided, but *one* thing is needful for our unity—the empathy and compassion of the living Son of God.

Surely there has not been another time in history when women have questioned their self-worth as harshly and critically as now. Many women are searching, almost frantically, as never before, for a sense of personal purpose and meaning. If I were Satan and wanted to destroy a society, I think I would stage a full-blown blitz on women. I would keep them so distraught and distracted that they would never find their calming strength and serenity.

Satan has effectively done that, catching us in the crunch of trying to be superhuman instead of striving to reach our unique, God-given potential within such diversity. He tauntingly teases us that if we don't have it all—fame, fortune, families, and fun, and have it all the time—we have been shortchanged and are second-class citizens in the race of life. Too many of us are struggling and suffering, too many are running faster than they have strength, expecting *too* much of themselves.

We *must* have the courage to be imperfect while striving for perfection. We can become so sidetracked in our compulsive search for identity and self-esteem that we really believe it *can* be found in having perfect figures or academic degrees or professional status or even absolute motherly success. Yet, in so searching externally, we can be torn from our true internal, eternal selves. We often worry so much about pleasing and performing for others that we lose our uniqueness—that full and relaxed acceptance of one's self as a person of worth and individuality. We become so frightened and insecure that we cannot be generous toward the diversity and individuality, and yes, problems, of our neighbors. Too many women with these anxieties watch helplessly as their lives unravel from the very core that centers and sustains them. Too many are like a ship at sea without sail or rudder, "tossed to and fro," as the Apostle Paul said (see Ephesians 4:14), until more and more of us are genuinely, rail-grabbingly seasick.

Where is the sureness that allows us to sail our ship, whatever winds may blow, with the master seaman's triumphant cry, "Steady as she goes"? Where is the inner stillness we so cherish?

I believe we can find our steady footing and stilling of the soul by turning away from physical preoccupations, superwoman accomplishments, and endless popularity contests, and returning instead to the wholeness of our soul, that unity in our very being that balances the demanding and inevitable diversity of life.

Often we fail to consider the glorious possibility within our own souls. We need to remember that divine promise, "The Kingdom of God is within you" (Luke 17:21). Perhaps we forget that the kingdom of God is within us because too much attention is given to this outer shell, this human body of ours, and the frail, too-flimsy world in which it moves.

Permit me to share with you an analogy that I created from something I read years ago. It helped me then—and helps me still—in my examination of inner strength and spiritual growth.

The analogy is of a soul—a human soul, with all of its splendor—being placed in a beautifully carved but very tightly locked box. Reigning in majesty and illuminating our soul in this innermost box is our Lord and our Redeemer, Jesus Christ, the living Son of the living God. This box is then placed—and locked—inside another, larger one, and so on until five beautifully carved but very securely locked boxes await the woman who is skillful and wise enough to open them. In order for her to have free communication with the Lord, she must find the key to and unlock the contents of these boxes. Success will then reveal to her the beauty and divinity of her own soul and her gifts and her grace as a daughter of God.

For me, *prayer* is the key to the first box. We kneel to ask for help for our tasks and then arise to find that the first lock is now open. But this ought not to seem just a convenient and contrived miracle, for if we are to search for real light and eternal certainties, we have to pray as the ancients prayed. The words most often used to describe urgent, prayerful labor are *wrestle, plead, cry,* and *hunger.* In some sense, prayer may be the hardest work we ever will engage in, and perhaps it should be. It is pivotal protection against becoming so involved with worldly possessions and honors and status that we no longer desire to undertake the search for our soul.

For those who, like Enos, pray in faith and gain entrance to a new dimension of their potential divinity, they are led to box number two. Here our prayers alone do not seem to be sufficient. We must turn to the scriptures for God's long-recorded teachings about our souls. We must learn. Surely every woman in this church is under divine obligation to learn and grow and develop. If the glory of God is intelligence, then learning, especially learning from the scriptures, stretches us toward Him.

I have discovered that if my own progress stalls, it stalls from malnutrition born of not eating and drinking daily from His holy writ. There have been challenges in my life that would have completely destroyed me had I not had the scriptures both on my bedstand and in my purse so that I could partake of them day and night at a moment's notice. So box two is opened through *learning from the scriptures.* I have discovered that by studying them I can have, again and again, an exhilarating encounter with God.

However, at the beginning of such success in emancipating the soul, Lucifer becomes more anxious, especially as we approach box number three. He knows that we are about to learn one very important and fundamental principle—that to truly find ourselves we must lose ourselves—so he begins to block our increased efforts to love God, our neighbor, and ourselves. Through the last decade, Satan has enticed all humanity to engage almost all of their energies in the pursuit of romantic love or thing-love or excessive self-love. In so doing, we forget that appropriate self-love and self-esteem are the promised reward for putting others first. "Whosoever shall seek to save his life shall lose it; and whosoever shall lose his life shall preserve it" (Luke 17:33). Box three opens only to the key of *charity.*

With charity, real growth and genuine insight begin. But the lid to box four seems nearly impossible to penetrate. Unfortunately, the faint-hearted and fearful often turn back here. The going seems too difficult, the lock too secure. This is a time for self-evaluation. To see ourselves as we really are often brings pain, but it is only through true humility, repentance, and renewal that we will come to know God. "Learn of me; for I am meek and lowly in heart," he said (Matthew 11:29). We must be patient with ourselves as we overcome weaknesses, and we must remember to rejoice over all that is good in us. This will strengthen our inner selves and leave us less dependent on outward acclaim. When our souls pay less attention to public praise, they then also care very little about public disapproval. Competition and jealousy and envy now begin to have no meaning. Just imagine the powerful spirit that would exist in our female society if we finally arrived at the point where, like our Savior, our real desire was to be counted as the *least* among our sisters. The rewards here are of such profound strength and quiet triumph of faith that we are carried into an even brighter sphere. So the fourth box, unlike the others, is broken open, just as a contrite heart is broken. *We are reborn*—like a flower growing and blooming out of the broken crust of the earth.

To share with you my feelings of opening the fifth box, I must compare the beauty of our souls with the holiness of our temples. There, in a setting not of this world, where fashions and position and professions go unrecognized, we have our chance to find peace and serenity and stillness that will anchor our soul forever, for there we may find God. For those of us who, like the brother of Jared, have the courage and faith to break through the veil into that sacred center of existence (see Ether 3:6–19), we will find the brightness of the final box brighter than the noonday sun. There we find wholeness—holiness. That is what it says over the entrance to the fifth box: *Holiness to the Lord.* "Know ye not that ye are the temple of God?" (1 Corinthians 3:16). I testify that you are holy—that divinity is abiding within you waiting to be uncovered—to be unleashed and magnified and demonstrated.

I have heard it said by some that the reason women in the Church struggle to know themselves is because they don't have a divine female role model. But we do. We believe we have a mother in heaven. May I quote from President Spencer W. Kimball in a general conference address:

> When we sing that doctrinal hymn . . . "O My Father," we get a sense of the ultimate in maternal modesty, of the restrained, queenly elegance of our Heavenly Mother, and knowing how profoundly our mortal mothers have shaped us here, do we suppose her influence on us as individuals to be less?[1]

I have never questioned why our mother in heaven seems veiled to us, for I believe the Lord has His reasons for revealing as little as He has on that subject. Furthermore, I believe we know much more about our eternal nature than we think we do, and it is our sacred obligation to express our knowledge, to teach it to our young sisters and daughters, and in so doing to strengthen their faith and help them through the counterfeit confusions of these difficult latter days. Let me point out some examples.

The Lord has not placed us in this lone and dreary world without a blueprint for living. In Doctrine and Covenants 52, we read the Lord's words: "I will give unto you a pattern in *all things, that ye may not be deceived*" (Doctrine and Covenants 52:14; emphasis added). He certainly includes us women in that promise. He has given us patterns in the Bible, the Book of Mormon, the Doctrine and Covenants, and the Pearl of Great Price; and he has given us patterns in the temple ceremony. As we study these patterns, we must continually ask, "Why does the Lord choose to say these particular words and present it in just this way?" We know he uses metaphors and symbols and parables and allegories to teach us of his eternal ways. We have all recognized the relationship between Abraham and Isaac that so parallels God's anguish over the sacrifice of his son, Jesus Christ. But, as women, do we stretch ourselves and also ask about Sarah's travail in this experience as well? We need to search in this manner, and we need always to look for deeper meaning. We should look for parallels and symbols. We should look for themes and motifs and repeated patterns.

One obvious pattern is that both the Bible and the Book of Mormon begin with a family theme, including family conflict. I have always believed this symbolized something eternal about *family* far more than just the story of those particular parents or those particular children. Surely all of us—married or single, with children and without—see something of Adam and Eve and something of Cain and Abel every day of our lives. With or without marriage, or with or without children, we all have some of the feelings of Lehi, Sariah, Laman, Nephi, Ruth, Naomi, Esther, the sons of Helaman, and the daughters of Ishmael.

Those are types and shadows for us, prefigurations of our own mortal joys and sorrows, just as Joseph and Mary are, in a sense, types and shadows of parental devotion as they nurtured the Son of God. These all seem to me to be symbols of higher principles and truths, symbols carefully chosen to show us the way, whether we are married or single, young or old, with family or without.

And, obviously, the temple is highly symbolic. May I share an experience I had there concerning the careful choice of words and symbols?

As I waited in the temple chapel, I sat next to an elderly man who unexpectedly but sweetly turned to me and said, "If you want a clear picture of the Creation, read Abraham 4." As I started to turn to Abraham, I just happened to brush past Moses 3:5: "For I, the Lord God, created all things, of which I have spoken, spiritually, before they were naturally upon the face of the earth." Another message of prefiguration—a spiritual pattern giving meaning to mortal creations. I then read Abraham 4 carefully and took the opportunity of going to an initiatory session. I left there with greater revelatory light on something I had always known in my heart to be so—that men *and* women are joint heirs of the blessings of the priesthood, and even though men bear the greater burden of administering it, women are not without their priesthood-related responsibilities.

Then, as I attended the endowment session, I asked myself if I were the Lord and could give my children on earth only a simplified but powerfully symbolic example of their roles and missions, how much would I give and where would I start? I listened to every word. I watched for patterns and prototypes.

I quote to you from Abraham 4:27: "So the Gods went down to organize man in their own image, in the image of the Gods to form they him, male *and* female, to form they *them*" (emphasis added). They formed male and they formed female—in the *image of the Gods,* in *their* own image.

Then, in a poignant exchange with God, Adam states that he will call the woman Eve. And why does he call her Eve? "Because she [is] the mother of all living" (Genesis 3:20; Moses 4:26).

As I tenderly acknowledge the very real pain that many single women, or married women who have not borne children, feel about any discussion of motherhood, could we consider this one possibility about our eternal female identity—our unity in our diversity? Eve was given the identity of "the mother of all living"—years, decades, perhaps centuries before she ever bore a child. It would appear that her *motherhood preceded her maternity,* just as surely as the perfection of the Garden preceded the struggles of mortality. I believe *mother* is one of those very carefully chosen words, one of those rich words—with meaning after meaning after meaning. We must not, at all costs, let that word divide us. I believe with all my heart that it is first and foremost a statement about our nature, not a head count of our children.

Some women give birth and raise children but never "mother" them. Others, whom I love with all my heart, "mother" all their lives but have never given birth. And all of us are Eve's daughters, whether we are married or single, maternal or barren. We are created in the image of the Gods to become gods and goddesses. And we can provide something of that divine pattern, that maternal prototype, for each other and for those who come after us. Whatever our circumstance, we can reach out, touch, hold, lift, and nurture—but we cannot do it in isolation. We need a community of sisters stilling the soul and binding the wounds of fragmentation.

I know that God loves us individually and collectively *as women,* and that he has a mission for every one of us. As I learned on my Galilean hillside, I testify that if our desires are righteous, God overrules for our good and that heavenly parents will tenderly attend to our needs. In our diversity and individuality, my prayer is that we will be united—united in seeking *our* specific, foreordained mission, united in asking *not,* "What can the kingdom do for me?" but

"What can I do for the kingdom? How can I fulfill the measure of *my* creation? In my circumstances and with my challenges and my faith, where is my *full* realization of the godly image in which I was created?"

With faith in God, his prophets, his church, and ourselves—with faith in our own divine creation—may we be peaceful and let go of our cares and troubles over so many things. May we believe—nothing doubting—in the light that shines, even in a dark place.

NOTES

Adapted from *Strength and Stillness: A Message for Women* (Deseret Book, 2015).

1. Spencer W. Kimball, "The True Way of Life and Salvation," *Ensign*, May 1978.

YOU WERE MADE FOR JOY

The Jews had light, and gladness, and joy, and honour.

And in every province, and in every city, whithersoever the king's commandment and his decree came, the Jews had joy and gladness, a feast and a good day. (Esther 8:16-17)

WE ARE HERE TO HAVE JOY

Lisa Valentine Clark

LISA VALENTINE CLARK is an author and host of the feel-good service show *Random Acts*. She headlined the musical improv TV show *Show Offs* on BYUtv and has starred in movies like *Stalking Santa*. She was a script consultant, producer, and actor in the film *Once I Was a Beehive*, and currently hosts the weekly podcast *The Lisa Show* on BYUradio. Lisa and her late husband Christopher have five children.

I want to address the philosophical and spiritual question: *Why joy?* Is this even something that is a worthy or acceptable pursuit? How do we find it when we are consumed by the harsh realities of our existence including the evil of our world, the detailed suffering of our sisters and brothers due to war, misogyny, racism, inequality, as well as our personal and family disappointments, sin, lost dreams, failures, illnesses, and grief?

Yes, I'm fun at parties.

The decision to live with joy requires us to be brave. It is a choice.

> True joy is not for the fainthearted. You must decide to be happy. Joy is an act of courage. Joy will not abide until you make a conscious decision to treasure it.[1]

It's easier to be jaded, sarcastic, over it, checked out. But we have been taught by a living prophet that joy is not conditional for the Lord. He wants us to find joy. President Russell M. Nelson taught, "When the focus of our lives is on . . . Jesus Christ and His gospel, we can feel joy regardless of what is happening—or not happening—in our lives. Joy comes from and because of Him. He is the source of all joy."[2]

It is interesting to me that President Nelson would talk about not only what is happening, but what is not happening, which I interpret as good desires—things we really want and deserve but might not get. I suspect that speaks to most of us. Not because we want too much, but because we have studied the gospel and have learned what good gifts to ask for.

So this brave decision, to live with joy, seems vague. But modern scripture tells us how: "I will impart unto you of my Spirit, which shall enlighten your mind, which shall fill your soul with joy" (Doctrine and Covenants 11:13). An enlightened, expansive mind (full of ideas and creativity) fills our soul—both body and spirit—with joy. It seems simple.

I have typically been an optimistic realist, a kind of Pollyanna type, from a mixture of genes and my environment growing up. But in the spring of 2016, my amazing, funny, lovely, smart, kind husband, Dr. Christopher Clark, was diagnosed with ALS, a terminal neurodegenerative disease with no treatments, no cure, and a life expectancy of two to five years. During that time, we had five kids living at home and from that moment on, not one aspect of my life was ever the same.

Oh yeah, I'm just jumping right into this. Because how can you really talk about living with joy without talking about how to choose to feel joy when you don't feel joyful, and you're struggling, and your personal circumstances are telling you it is impossible?

Christopher lived with the disease for four and a half years and during that time span, he went from a weird twitch in his leg to not being able to move or speak at the time of his death. That's a lot of change.

After Christopher died, it felt like the lights went out. I describe it as a sad montage in a movie. You know the montages they have in films to get through a year or two? Fast forward and it's just a lot of brown-sepia toned film of a sad woman eating soup by a window as the rain trickles down the pane. That's how I see it: it's my soup-eating montage phase of life.

Showing up, getting up, getting dressed, putting on my lipstick and going to work, calling friends, trying to create—a show, a movie, an event, anything—being present with my kids, seeing the sun, trying at life, all of those things were things I had never had to practice before. It's been humbling and exhausting.

And I've been blessed. I've had my best moments because I've chosen to. Looking back, I've laughed the hardest and experienced moments of joy and love because I did a lot of things I didn't initially want to do (or think I could). No one who knows me superficially would suspect how difficult this has been. But here we are.

Through these experiences of "before" the illness, when inviting joy into my life was fun and seemed effortless; "during" the illness, when joy was a little more calculated and tricky but still abundant; and the "after" times, when inviting joy is an entirely different mindset; living with joy has been different during each of those stages. Here is what I've learned: Joy is a creative act, not a formula.

It can be very difficult to move forward, joyfully creating, when you have certain parameters like terminal diseases, taxes, and bad timing. It can feel like your calling to live in the world at this time is less-than-divine. But it *is* a divine calling and, like Elder Richard G. Scott said,

> Sadness, disappointment, and severe challenge are events in life, not life itself. I do not minimize how hard some of these events are. They can extend over a long period of time, but they should not be allowed to become the confining center of everything you do. The Lord inspired Lehi to declare the fundamental truth, "Men are, that they might have joy." That is a conditional statement: "they might have joy." It is not conditional for the Lord. His intent is that each of us finds joy. It will not be conditional for you as you obey the commandments, have faith in the Master, and do the things that are necessary to have joy here on earth.[3]

Inviting joy, like creativity itself, is a creative act. We need to think of it in creative terms. Like any artistic endeavor, we need tools, and we need to find our flow to let it happen.

Sometimes, we unknowingly limit ourselves and what we think is possible in our work, in our homes, in our lives. We do that for good reason—we have limited resources including budgets, energy, and time. But the first step of creativity is opening our minds to what might be possible, in a way we have never considered. We brainstorm before we write, for example. If we start editing our ideas, our punctuation, whatever, during the brainstorm, we alter the outcome. We limit the effectiveness. We have to first dream. Creating our lives—how we invite joy—is no different. Here's some poetic inspiration that got my mind to just imagine that one day I might have hope for a happy life:

> What if there is a path for you that is greater than what you can envision? What if there is a life for you that is more than you would even know to ask for? What if you are inherently and unknowingly limited by your old perspectives, your outdated ideas of what is possible? What if all the discomfort within your being is simply trying to redirect you to a place beyond anything you've considered before? What if there is more than you know? What if there arc things out there so good, you don't even know you're waiting for them?[4]

When I had no hope for a happy future or for light, I held on to the idea of God's mysterious, creative love for me, and the expression of that love isn't something I can predict in specific terms.

When I had no hope, I borrowed some from other hope-filled friends. I pleaded to God to help me find some.

I chose joy when I was in the middle of a ridiculous situation. I was asked to do the impossible: prepare Chris, my beloved, to die, and convince him we would be okay—giving him a "good death" *all* while I prepared my children and helped them deal with this life-altering, profound loss, while I was in the depths of the worst grief and pain I'd ever known, all during a global pandemic that kept me isolated from my support group and help. It was impossible. It was, frankly, pretty ridiculous.

We felt moments of joy during our pain. I felt strength from the Spirit in an undeniable way. I can't say that I always focused on the joy, but we laughed a lot as Christopher died. Some of his final words were a joke that, when I remember it, still makes me laugh. We give thanks for the undeniable blessings that we all saw. It was impossible and we were carried through, so much so that I wish I were still living in it. I felt moments of such intense, overwhelming love and joy that I didn't know if I could physically hold it all.

Had you asked me at the beginning of the pandemic, "Well, how are you going to take care of Chris without any CNAs, nurses, therapists, or help?" I didn't know. It was impossible. I couldn't lift him up by myself. He needed twenty-four-hour care. He couldn't scratch his nose by himself. I was working full-time, still going in super early during the pandemic to provide for our family, while taking care of five children at home who were depressed or mad or apathetic (and rightfully so).

I felt like how the people of Alma are described in Mosiah when they were being persecuted by the former priests of Noah:

> Lift up your heads and be of good comfort. . . . And I will . . . ease the burdens which are put upon your shoulders, that even you cannot feel them upon your backs, even while you are in bondage; and this will I do that ye may stand as witnesses for me hereafter, and that ye may know of a surety that I, the Lord God, do visit my people in their afflictions. (Mosiah 24:13–14)

I was given the power to function on little sleep, work in a new job and a brand-new career, take care of Christopher, pick him up, bathe him, feed him, administer emergency medicine to him, comfort my children, pay the bills, and have joy around me. It doesn't make sense. We did it. Sometimes I have to remind myself that it happened. It was not my plan, but it was a series of miracles. It was a happy, joyful time. For our family, creating a new reality amid a dramatic backdrop of illness was another creative pursuit, like producing or directing a play, putting on an improvisational musical, or playing a song on the piano. Elder Scott continued:

> Being creative will help you enjoy life. It engenders a spirit of gratitude. It develops latent talent, sharpens your capacity to reason, to act, and to find purpose in life. It dispels loneliness and heartache. It gives a renewal, a spark of enthusiasm, and zest for life.[5]

This is how my late husband lived Elder Scott's words:

- When he was diagnosed, I was at a loss about what to do next, as in, that day. Christopher suggested we live our lives. You know, go to work, raise our kids, laugh with our friends.

That didn't feel right to me, and I told him so. He said, "What are we going to do, stay in bed and cry all day?" I replied, "Uh, yeah . . . actually that's exactly what I want to do." He told me I could obviously do whatever I wanted, but he was going to keep on living. And he did.

- Christopher had a really good therapist who gave us some great advice: "Give yourself ten to fifteen minutes a day to feel sorry for yourself. Feel really horrible about your situation, and then when it's over, get on with your day." Christopher needed those minutes early on, but after a while, he didn't.
- With each new stage, each new adjustment, Christopher said, "I'll focus on what I can do," and he did. When he couldn't play the piano, he focused on directing plays and teaching. When he couldn't speak, he focused on writing and producing. His life was constant creative focus, not regret.
- He continued embarrassing kids in public places. There were prerecorded phrases on his adaptive speech device like, "Help, I don't know this person!" and he would play them in public with his kids, who would roll their eyes and say, "Dad, please . . . don't."
- Christopher never stopped reaching out to people, encouraging them, and laughing with them. He started the day with the thought and the prayer, "Who can I help today?"
- Instead of worrying about how much time he had, Christopher would remind us "I'm still here," and remind us that he trusted this was God's plan for him. He would say, "This is my path. This is what God intended for me, so I can do it. I'll endure to the end. I feel like George Bailey—the luckiest

man on earth with the best friends and family." His life oozed with creativity and he invited the Spirit in his pursuit of a happy, joyful life. It is not coincidence that he was creating something, many things, until his last day on earth. He created joy not just for himself, but for others, especially for me and our children.

Christopher focused on the here and now and tried not to compare his life to others, and as a result, he was happy and felt purposeful under the worst of human conditions. This is possible by living in the moment, by appreciating and savoring the ordinary days. And I am convinced that if you are not present in your life today, you will miss the joy as it happens.

I am an improviser by profession and personality. Being present in improv is everything—that's how you create a story, characters, laughter, tension, and beauty. It's also how you create joy. You step onstage not knowing what you're going to say or do, but you are present—listening, believing, and practicing with other players. You have to interact, trust each other, and really listen to each other. That moves the story forward.

In improvisation, you make up everything as you go. In the moment, and by listening to other people on stage, you make up character traits, movement, and dialogue. It might be a simple scene, or an entire original play or musical. You might be thinking, "This sounds horrible." But, to some extent, it's something all of us do every day. The guiding principle of improv is "Yes, and . . ." It means that you accept whatever is offered to you onstage and add something to it. That's it. You don't deny it or question it, you just take it and move forward.

For example, someone starts an action onstage, like a big stirring motion, and they're thinking, "I'm a baker mixing a cake." Another actor enters the stage, interprets the action in a split second, and adds something to it. They may, for example, interpret the stirring movement as a witch stirring a bubbling brew, and so they say, "I brought the eye of newt to finish the potion!" They've accepted the offering of the stirring movement, and they've added to it by adding more information for the scene to build—we are witches making a brew and it's almost finished. An example of not doing that is saying, "What are you talking about? I'm baking a cake, not a potion!" That's denying the reality of the moment ("This is not happening") and adding nothing. You're back to square one and the audience and other actor are uncomfortable. It's boring.

Accepting your offering in life and adding to it, even if the offering is dumb, is vital. Even if you really, really wanted to play a baker in this scene and had ideas for a storyline and characters, if you hold onto that idea instead of accepting what's actually happening, not only are you a selfish scene partner, but it doesn't create anything but confusion. If, on the other hand, you accept the offering, even (and maybe especially) when you don't want it, and add something to it—anything—you are playing, creating. It is interesting, oftentimes extremely funny, and it moves the scene ahead in a way you could never predict.

When we were first married, my late husband took a career aptitude test at BYU to help him decide what profession he should go into. He was almost done with his degree and didn't know what to do next, so we were really excited when we found out the results were ready—as if this would tell us exactly what we needed to know. Christopher went into the career counselor's office, excited to see what direction it would scientifically reveal . . . and she was visibly upset. She immediately said, "This has never happened before." He said, "What is it? I'm ready! What's the answer?" She went on to explain, again, very nervously, "Well, this is just an idea. I mean, it's not definitive. It's just an idea." He repeated, "What does it say?!" She hesitated and replied, "Your number one job suggestion is . . . circus performer."

Huh. It wasn't a joke. He didn't laugh. When he told me, I didn't laugh. We thought, Yeah, that tracks. It actually makes sense. And because I think he was expecting "lawyer," or something like that, the future felt unknown because we had to accept that that *was* a good career choice for Christopher, but . . . then what? What came next was going into acting and directing with additional degrees and training in Shakespeare, teaching, improv, and acting techniques from all over the world. Ultimately, he became the chair of the theater department at UVU until his terminal disease robbed his voice, and at that time Christopher admitted, "It does very much feel like I'm running a three-ring circus." This story is what I think about when I suggest you should accept your reality now and move forward with it, not in spite of it.

Our prophet, President Russell M. Nelson, said:

> Clearly, Lehi knew opposition, anxiety, heartache, pain, disappointment, and sorrow. Yet he declared boldly and without reservation a principle as revealed by the Lord: "Men are, that they might have joy." Imagine! Of all the words he could have used to describe the nature and

purpose of our lives here in mortality, he chose the word joy!

Life is filled with detours and dead ends, trials and challenges of every kind. Each of us has likely had times when distress, anguish, and despair almost consumed us. Yet we are here to have joy?

Yes! The answer is a resounding yes![6]

Of all the words he could have used to describe why we're here and what it all means, he chose the word *joy*. From disappointments like a confusing career test to the all-consuming sorrow of a terminal illness, God's intent for us is joy. I have learned that the present, here and now, is where we create joy. After all, timing is everything.

Those familiar with grief, for example, know that you have to sit with it in the present, to live with it. You can't dismiss it, repress it, hide it, stifle it. You've got to face it, befriend it, learn to live with it, share it—that is how you carry it. You need to be present in order to do that. You have to find others to be present with as well.

To truly live the gospel, you need to be present. You need to be present and honest with the Lord to truly have your heart changed. You can experience joy, but maybe not in the way you think you can. It becomes something new.

You know the difference between functioning and *living*. Responding (which is necessary at times) and acting are not the same. Living with joy is not just a byproduct of "choosing good" or making good choices, but it *is* the thing in and of itself. If it's hard to do (and a lot of times it is), then maybe we need to rest, maybe we need to repent, and maybe we need to wake up and act on our desires. Personal revelation and following the Spirit enlighten our mind as to what to do. This is why developing personal revelation and a relationship with the Spirit is so important: because our circumstances and our needs change. Being present in our lives, really accepting what our life actually is, rather than what we wish it were, and in some cases, what it used to be, isn't real or helpful.

Just like in improv, accepting our offering and not judging it helps us see what it is and then we can add to it to move the scene, our lives, forward, in order to create something new—something real.

The most effective way to create joy, I have found, is to fast-track it with gratitude.

A gratitude practice is one of the best ways to invite joy. I know how to invite anxiety and sorrow. I am very good at hurting my own feelings. Here's how I do it: I imagine things that don't exist. I imagine them so often, so automatically, that I start to believe them as if they were true. I imagine what people think of me, or I replay horrible events that have happened to me over and over again. Basically, I look for reasons to support my most useless thoughts. I don't want to brag, but trauma and grief have made me an expert at this practice. Can I cry on demand? Oh, come on!

Inviting joy is much like inviting an honored guest to your home. You really hope they show up, but you're not sure. So you have to incentivize it. You promise good things—good food, good company, whatever you can, and then you hope.

In anticipation of some horrible events in my life, when I was in the thick of caregiving sad children and a dying husband during a global pandemic, I made a list of "things I should do to not lose my mind and slip into the horrible, dark abyss." They included things like get sunlight, drink more water, exercise, get regular sleep, eat more vegetables, get a therapist, take medication, pray, stay connected to friends, etc. I knew that if I went down, no one in my family would survive. And I had heard and read over and over about the benefits of gratitude, so I decided to keep a gratitude journal during worst time of my life. Every day, I listed five things at the end of the day, all new, little or big, that I was truly grateful for.

I was desperate, and I practiced this every day—even on the worst days, the days when a pricey piece of adaptive handicapped equipment wasn't covered by insurance, even when one of my kids came to me horribly depressed, even when I felt like a failure at work, or when my late husband lost more movement, even when he started sleeping more, or having bigger symptoms, or when I realized things I had already lost that I hadn't noticed, like most of my dreams for the future. Even those days, I kept a gratitude journal, because *what did I have to lose?*

That journal included a lot of entries about food. (It was then that my appreciation of the perfect chicken sandwich really flourished.) I learned that small moments of appreciation can change your life. They changed mine, because we find what we're looking for and what we direct our thoughts to. President Russell M. Nelson taught, "When the focus of our lives is on . . . Jesus Christ and His gospel, we can feel joy regardless of what is happening—or not happening—in our lives. Joy comes from and because of Him. He is the source of all joy."[7]

We don't have to be loyal to feelings of depression, anxiety, sorrow, even and especially when they are so strong. We can feel those things *and* feel joy, feel happy, find something really funny, and feel God's love for us, too.

The practice of gratitude brings deep joy for us amid our trials (and whether they go away or not). It trains us to look for the unexpected good all around it. It quiets our mind amid injustice, pain, and grief, and it offers us real retreat and balm when we need it the very most.

If you don't feel grateful in hard times, I get you. I understand. Trauma, pain, disappointment, and heartache scientifically make it difficult for us to experience joy. But gratitude makes us mentally and physically healthier, it reduces stress, it literally changes the neural pathways in our brain so we are more likely to see the good in the world. It benefits our relationships and deepens our satisfaction in life. It is prescribed all the time for depression and anxiety. For those familiar with depression, anxiety, grief, or intrusive thoughts, we know that practicing to train our brains and hold onto every good thought is sometimes hard work.

Initially, I didn't fully understand the practice of gratitude as a creative pursuit, but of course it is. If we want to emulate our heavenly parents and "see things as they really are" (as Jacob 4 teaches), we need to expand our minds, which requires us to practice. Creative Rick Rubin says:

> *The ability to look deeply*
> *is the root of creativity.*
> *To see past the ordinary and mundane*
> *and get to what might otherwise be invisible.*[8]

The creative art of gratitude, not just recognizing it but practicing it, is an invitation to the Spirit. Letting that practice enlighten our minds is an opportunity for the Spirit to turn our attention and focus to our Savior. The good news of the gospel, the life and teachings of Jesus Christ, are an invitation for joy to come into our lives. The Spirit helps us remember and see things as they really are.

> For the Spirit speaketh the truth and lieth not. Wherefore, it speaketh of things as they really are, and of things as they really will be; wherefore, these things are manifested unto us plainly, for the salvation of our souls. But behold, we are not witnesses alone in these things; for God also spake them unto prophets of old. (Jacob 4:13)

My favorite gratitude journal entry was one that I wrote on the night my husband died. It is sacred to me now. I was grateful that night for eternally significant truths and experiences that I hadn't really seen before. Those truths that the Spirit taught me prepared me for an even harder time of life: life without Christopher. The Spirit speaketh the truth, of things as they really are, and of things as they really will be, and that gave me joy in a way I hadn't anticipated I could have.

It is brave thing to choose joy, but we can practice joy by living in the present and using gratitude to create more joy. These creative arts and the way we practice them will create joy not just for ourselves, but for others. Joy is intended for us, or, like our prophet tells us:

> Life is filled with detours and dead ends, trials and challenges of every kind . . . times when distress, anguish,

and despair almost consumed us. Yet we are here to have joy? Yes! The answer is a resounding yes![9]

NOTES

Adapted from a talk given at BYU Women's Conference.

1. Elaine S. Marshall, "In This Life I Shall Have Joy," Brigham Young University Devotional, April 30, 2004.
2. Russell M. Nelson, "Joy and Spiritual Survival," *Ensign* or *Liahona*, November 2016.
3. Richard G. Scott, "Finding Joy in Life," *Ensign* or *Liahona*, May 1996.
4. Brianna Wiest, *When You're Ready, This Is How You Heal* (New York: Thought Catalog Books, 2022).
5. Richard G. Scott, "Finding Joy in Life."
6. Russell M. Nelson, "Joy and Spiritual Survival."
7. Russell M. Nelson, "Joy and Spiritual Survival."
8. Rick Rubin, *The Creative Act: A Way of Being* (New York: Penguin Press, 2023).
9. Russell M. Nelson, "Joy and Spiritual Survival."